Bingo Boys and Poodle-Fakers

Chonkey
Jay
Biffin
Umpty-poo
Loonslatt
Gnark

Squffer
Jagger
Gobbin
Flotch

Bingo Boys
and Poodle-Fakers

A CURIOUS COMPENDIUM OF
HISTORICAL SLANG

Collected from the best authorities

WITH DECORATIONS BY
Clare Mackie

LONDON

The Folio Society

2007

TYPESET AT THE FOLIO SOCIETY IN BELL.
PRINTED AND BOUND BY GRAFOS S.A.,
BARCELONA, SPAIN.

'The past is a foreign country: they do things differently there.' When L. P. Hartley penned his famous maxim over half a century ago, it is unlikely that language was at the forefront of his mind. Yet even the barest acquaintance with the colloquial speech of other times can leave one with the disorientating feeling of being a foreigner in one's own land. When Dickens or Shakespeare, Fielding or Wodehouse wanted to conjure a world outside the experience of their polite readers, to give their characters an air of edgy authenticity and imbue their narratives with an illicit thrill, they nonchalantly spiced their pages with slang terms and phrases that bewildered all but the most hardened aficionados then and now. Historical novelists, like all good genre writers, have knowingly thrived on the same trick. From Georgette Heyer to George Macdonald Fraser, their novels echo to the evocative clamour of cramp language and flash patter.

But, like any foreign language, historical slang repays closer study for what it reveals about society's subconscious, its distinctive preoccupations and obsessions, fears and peccadilloes. For example, it is commonly believed that the Inuit need dozens of different words for snow. What, then, does it say about the English that their way of life once demanded over one hundred terms for gin? Drugs nowadays provide the same fertile mulch to feed slang's appetite for endless invention. The 'liquid madness' that was gin has surrendered its pre-eminence on the pedestal of illegal vices and social ills to crystal meth and crack cocaine.

Thought about in this way, historical slang becomes the auditory equivalent of a good cartoon. Because it is highly coloured, deliberately transgressive and unabashedly distorted, it can provide a more vividly true-to-life picture of those aspects of the past which are beneath the dignity of art and literate and conventional history to notice. The effect is rather like reading a guidebook to a strange city before stepping outside one's hotel room to experience the invigorating assault of sights, smells and sounds which provide one's most lasting impressions of a foreign place.

Observed through its slang, historical Britain appears very different to the familiar picture. It is an alien world we encounter, ever alert to the comic possibilities of revolting schoolboys, unusual trousers and robbery with violence. It is a world which makes its own entertainment, and finds it in the strangest places: in public executions, in fashions in facial hair, in the foibles of farm animals, in unconventional foodstuffs and in the inhabitants of Bristol. A world in which people appear not as they would like to be but as they more often are: finding amusement in others' misfortunes and inadequacies, teasing those visibly different from themselves, laughing at others' physical failings, moral shortcomings and social faux pas.

Perhaps not so foreign a country after all.

The primary purpose of this brief compendium is to amuse and entertain. It is too short to be anything other than highly partial, both in the slang terms and phrases that are featured and in the definitions given. Allowing for the uncertainty which surrounds the origins, precise meanings and dates for such ephemeral language, precedence has been given to words and meanings now redundant and no longer widely known. Etymologies are given only occasionally: a large part of the amusement of historical slang comes from trying to decipher the often bizarre thought processes which gave rise to it.

Other than that, the coverage is as wide as possible within the Anglophone world. It reaches from Shakespearean England to the Second World War, and represents a multitude of forms: Mumpers' talk, Pedlars' French and thieves' cant, society slang, schoolboy jargon, circus patois and the distinctive argots of soldiers, sailors and Oxbridge students, amongst others. While British idiom necessarily predominates, it is leavened with a smattering of Australian, New Zealand and North American examples. Some are terms which emigrated with colonists, often to live on long after they had died out in their homeland. Others evolved to reflect the unique circumstances and challenges of life on the other side of the world.

Much of what would now be regarded as racist, obscene or otherwise offensive has been excluded. But it is not possible to avoid this territory altogether, without misrepresenting the past. Over two hundred years ago, that doyen of slang lexicographers, Francis Grose, wrestled with the same dilemma. One can do no better than repeat his plea for a degree of broad-mindedness in his readers:

> To prevent any charge of immorality being brought against this work, the Editor begs leave to observe, that when an indelicate or immodest word has obtruded itself for explanation, he has endeavoured to get rid of it in the most decent manner possible; and none have been admitted but such, as either could not be left out without rendering the work incomplete, or in some measure compensate by their wit for the trespass committed on decorum.

It should go without saying that the publishers do not endorse any of the sentiments expressed in the remainder of this volume. But it can only be hoped that what follows does not disclose too obviously the editor's own particular compulsions.

Baker, Aus. Sidney J. Baker, *A Popular Dictionary of Australian Slang* (Robertson and Mullens: Melbourne, 1943).

Baker, nz. Sidney J. Baker, *New Zealand Slang* (Whitcombe and Tombs: Christchurch, 1941).

B.E. 'B.E. Gent.', *A New Dictionary of the Terms Ancient and Modern of the Canting Crew, in its Several Tribes, of Gypsies, Beggers, Thieves, Cheats, etc.* (W. Hawes: London, c.1698).

Bee. 'Jon Bee' [John Badcock], *Slang: A Dictionary of the Turf, the Ring, the Chase, the Pit, of Bon-Ton, and the Varieties of Life* (T. Hughes: London, 1823).

Bowen. Frank C. Bowen, *Sea Slang* (Sampson Low: London, 1929).

Brandon. H. Brandon, 'A Dictionary of the Flash or Cant Language, Known to Every Thief and Beggar' (1839). Reprinted in Ducange.

Ducange. 'Ducange Anglicus', *The Vulgar Tongue: Comprising Two Glossaries of Slang, Cant, and Flash Words and Phrases, Principally Used in London at the Present Day* (B. Quaritch: London, 1857).

Egan. Pierce Egan, *Grose's Classical Dictionary of the Vulgar Tongue, Revised and Corrected, With the Addition of Numerous Slang Phrases Collected from Tried Authorities* (Sherwood, Neely and Jones: London, 1823).

Forces' Slang. Eric Partridge, ed., *A Dictionary of Forces' Slang 1939–1945* (Secker and Warburg: London, 1948).

Green. Jonathon Green, *Cassell's Dictionary of Slang* (Cassell: London, 1998).

Grose. Francis Grose, *A Classical Dictionary of the Vulgar Tongue* (S. Hooper: London, 1785).

Harman. Thomas Harman, *A Caveat or Warening for Common Cursetors* (1567). Reprinted in Robert Greene, *The Groundworke of Conny-Catching* (W. Barley: London, 1592).

Hotten. J. C. Hotten, *The Slang Dictionary: Etymological, Historical and Anecdotal* (Chatto and Windus: London, 1874).

Irwin. Godfrey Irwin, *American Tramp and Underworld Slang* (Scholartis Press: London, 1931).

Lex.Bal. *Lexicon Balatronicum: A Dictionary of Buckish Slang, University Wit, and Pickpocket Eloquence* (C. Chappel: London, 1811).

Partridge. Eric Partridge, *The Penguin Dictionary of Historical Slang*, ed. Jacqueline Simpson (Penguin: Harmondsworth, 1972).

Slang. Eric Partridge, *Slang Today and Yesterday, with a Short Historical Sketch and Vocabularies of English, American, and Australian Slang* (G. Routledge: London, 1933).

Soldierman. 'Soldierman', *Soldiers in Training: Advice and Hints for Young Soldiers, with Traditional Bugle Calls and Slang Vocabulary* (F. Warne: London, 1939).

Soldiers' Slang. John Brophy and Eric Partridge, 'Soldiers' Slang', in their *The Long Trail: What the British Soldier Sang and Said in the Great War of 1914–18* (André Deutsch: London, 1965).

Ware. J. Redding Ware, *Passing English of the Victorian Era* (G. Routledge: London, 1909).

War Slang. *The Soldiers' War Slang Dictionary: A List of Words and Phrases Used by British Soldiers in the Great War 1914–1918* (T. Werner Laurie: London, 1939).

Weseen. Maurice H. Weseen, *A Dictionary of American Slang* (G. G. Harrap: London, 1935).

Abandannad. A stealer of handkerchiefs. L18–M19.

Abandoned habits. The attire of Hyde Park *demi-mondaines.* M–L19.

Abbey lubber. An indolent monk. M16–M18.

Abishag. The illegitimate offspring of a woman seduced by someone else's husband. M–L19.

Abram man. One who impersonates a madman. M16–E18.

Abstain from beans. Retire from public life. E–M20.

Academy headache. The feeling produced by having to spend too much time at art exhibitions. L19.

Accrue chocolate. Curry favour; brown-nose. E–M20.

Acid drop. A constantly moaning or arguing sailor. E–M20.

Acrobat. A drinking glass, i.e. a tumbler. L19–E20.

Adam and Eve on a raft. Poached eggs on toast. E–M20.

Admiral of the Narrow Seas. 'One who from drunkenness vomits into the lap of the person sitting opposite to him' (*Lex.Bal.*). 17–M19. See *Vice Admiral of the Narrow Seas.*

Advertistics. 'Statistics' to promote products (US). E–M20.

Aetna. A bijou tea-making device. M–L19.

Affygraphy, fit to an, i.e. precisely, to a T. M19–E20.

Afternoon farmer. A virtuoso procrastinator. M19–E20.

1

Air. Air-hole. A small public park located on the site of a former church graveyard in a large town. L19–E20. *Air the dairy.* Expose one's breasts in public. 18–19.

Alberts. 'Toe rags as worn by dead-beats and tramps of low degree' (Baker, Aus.). 19–E20.

Alderman. A roast turkey trimmed with sausages. L18–E20.

Alexandra limp. 'An affected manner of walking seen for several years amongst women' (Ware). M–L19.

Algerine. A penurious individual who persists in borrowing trifling amounts of money. M–L19.

All nations. 'A composition of all the different spirits sold in a dram shop, collected in a vessel, into which the drainings of the bottles and quartern pots are emptied' (Grose). L18–E19.

Alsatian. A member of the London underworld. 18–19.

Alter the jeff's click. Make an item of clothing that wilfully disregards the customer's measurements. L19–E20.

Ambidexter. 'A lawyer that takes fees of plaintiff and defendant at once' (B.E.). 16–19.

Amen. Amen corner. The front pews of a church, populated by the most enthusiastically vocal worshippers (US). E20. *Amen snorter.* An Australian clergyman. L19.

Amuse. Throw snuff in the face of someone you intend to rob. L17–18.

Anabaptist. A careless pickpocket who has been the recipient of summary justice in the form of a ducking. L18–E19.

Anarchists. Safety matches (AUS). L19–E20.

Angel. Angel face. An innocently boyish flying officer (WWI). E20. *Angel maker.* A baby-farmer. M–L19. See also *Oil of angels.*

Angler. A petty thief specialising in the robbing of shop windows with a hooked stick. M16–E19.

Ankle-beater. A small boy who drives beasts to slaughter. 19.

Ann-chovey. A female shopkeeper. M19.

Annual. A bath (AUS). L19–E20.

Antidote. 'A very homely woman' (B.E.). L17–M18.

Anti-guggler. The tube used to suck the monkey (q.v.). L18.

Anythingarian. An individual bland enough not to hold a single decided opinion. E18–19.

Ape's paternoster. The chattering noise one makes when cold. E17–L19.

Apostles, manoeuvre the. Take out more credit in order to pay off one's debts, i.e. rob Peter to pay Paul. M18–E20.

Apricock water. Gin. M18.

Arack. An ardent spirit from the East Indies, sometimes distilled from fish roe – 'best when old' (B.E.). L17.

Arfarfanarf. Intoxicated. M19–E20.

Arse. Arse-foot. A penguin. L16–M19. *Arse-worm.* 'A little diminutive fellow' (B.E.). L17–18. *Ask* (or *Ax*) *my arse.* 'A common reply to any question; still deemed wit at sea' (*Lex.Bal.*). M18–20. *Hang an arse.* Stand back nervously; bring up the rear. 17–E20. *Lend one's arse and shite through one's ribs.* Lend money carelessly. L18–M19. *My arse on a bandbox.* The response to an offer of anything not fit for purpose. L18–M19. See also *Grease a fat sow in the arse; Hopper-arsed; Satchel-arsed fellow; Split-arsing; Tin-arsed; Wet arse and no fish.*

Arty-and-crafty. Neither useful nor comfortable. E20.

Athanasian wench. An easy lay (from the opening words of the Athanasian Creed, 'Whoever desires …'). 18–E19.

Attaboy. An American soldier (WWI). E20.

Auntycedents. Relatives on the mother's side (US). E20.

Australian flag. A protruding shirt-tail (AUS). L19–E20.

Autem. A church. M16–18. *Autem bawler.* A clergyman. 17–18. *Autem diver.* 1. A pickpocket who operates in churches. 17–18. 2. A churchwarden. 17–18. 3. A Baptist. 17–18. *Autem gogler.* A false prophet from France. 17–18.

Avoirdupois lay. The art of stealing the brass weights from shop counters. L18–M19.

Awkward squad. A body of inexperienced or uncoordinated soldiers given extra drill or weapons training. L19–M20.

Babe. A fat baseball player (US). E–M20. *Babes in the wood.* Offenders standing in the stocks. L18–E19. *The babes.* Anything particularly splendid. E20.

Baby. A tame puma (US). E20. *Baby's publichouse.* 'Nature's fount' (Ware). L19. *Have a baby.* Panic (WWII). M20.

Bacca-pipes. Facial hair ornamentally arranged into ringlets. M–L19.

Back. Back-hairing. 'Feminine fighting, in which the occipital locks suffer severely' (Ware). L19–E20. *Back-slang it.* Take a circuitous detour in order to avoid a person or place. E–M19.

Backgammon player. 'A fellow whose propensities lie out of the natural order of things in England' (Bee). M18–E19.

Badger. 1. A violent waterside robber who uses the river to dispose of his victims. E18–E19. 2. A mediocre rugby player. L19. *Badger game.* 'A blackmailing scheme … in which the victim is taken to a room or apartment by the woman accomplice, and there discovered by the "husband" ' (Irwin) (US). E–M20. *Badger-legged.* Owning one leg longer than the other. E18–E20. *Overdraw the badger.* Exceed one's overdraft. M19–E20.

Bad shag. 'No able woman's man' (*Lex.Bal.*). L18–M19.

Bag. Bag daddy. A female student's escort to social functions (US). M20. *Bagging.* A snack between meals. 18–19. *Have the bags off.* Live off one's private income. L19.

Baker-knee'd. 'One whose knees knock together in walking, as if kneading dough' (*Lex.Bal.*). 18–19.

Balaclava. A majestically large beard. M–L19.

Balderdash. 1. An 'ill, unpleasant, unwholesome mixture of wine, ale, etc.' (B.E.). L17–E19. 2. Lewd conversation. L18–E19.

Bald-headed butter. 'Butter free from hairs' (Ware). L19–E20.

Ballarat lantern. The stub of a candle in a broken bottle-neck (AUS). L19–E20.

Ballocks. 'A vulgar nickname for a parson' (*Lex.Bal.*). L17–E19.

Ballyhooly. Egregious overstatement by politicians and advertisers. E20.

Balum rancum. A dance in which all the female participants are prostitutes. 'NB The company dance in their birthday suits' (*Lex.Bal.*). M17–M19.

Bandicoot. Steal potatoes without disturbing the leafy part of the plant (AUS). 20.

Bandook. A musket or rifle. 18–E20.

Bang. Bang and biff. Syphilis (US). M20. *Banging.* Big, great; a term of approbation. 18–19. *Bang straw.* A farmer's servant. L18. See also under *Elephant.*

Bankrupt cart. A one-horse carriage. L18.

Banyan party. A sailors' picnic excursion. M19–E20.

Banzai party. A group of seamen hell-bent on enjoying their shore-leave. E20.

Bapper. A baker. M19–M20.

Barber. As common as a barber's chair in which a whole parish has sat to be trimmed. An expression used when referring to a popular prostitute. M16–M19. *Barber's sign.* The male genitalia: 'a standing pole and two wash balls' (*Lex.Bal.*). L18–19.

Barge. A breast enlargement imported from France. L19.

Barnacle. 1. A swindler. L16–E17. 2. An individual with a very nasal voice. M16–M17. 3. A good job or meal, easily obtained. L17–18.

Barrier blight. The state of apathy brought on at the prospect of exploring beyond the Antarctic ice-barrier. E20.

Bartholomew baby. A woman dressed in cheap flashy clothes. L17–E19.

Baseball. Small or insignificant. L19–E20.

Basket-making. 'Copulation, or making feet for children's stockings' (Grose). M18–E19.

Bastardly gullion. The illegitimate child of someone born out of wedlock: a bastard's bastard. L18–E19.

Bat. A cheap whore, 'so called from moving out like bats in the dusk of the evening' (*Lex.Bal.*). 17–E19.

Batchy. Daft, insane, in a funk (WWI, WWII). E–M20.

Bathmat. A duckboard (WWI). E20.

Batter the privates. Beg from door to door (US). E–M20.

Battle. Battle bag. A dirigible airship (WWI). E20. *Battle bowler.* A steel helmet (WWI, WWII). E–M20. *Battle cruiser.* A public house. M20. *Battle dress.* Pyjamas (WWII). M20.

Battledore-boy. A child learning his alphabet. L17–M18.

Batty-fanging. A drubbing. 19.

Bawker. An individual so far beyond the pale that he will sink to cheating at bowls. L16–E17.

Bay fever. 'A term of ridicule applied to convicts, who sham illness, to avoid being sent to Botany Bay' (*Lex.Bal.*). 19.

Bazaar. Rob, from 'the extortion practised by remorseless, smiling English ladies at bazaars' (Ware). L19–E20.

Beanpea. An effeminate young man. L19–E20.

Bear. Carry bear. Perform a mundane, unpleasant task. 19. *Loaded for bear.* Well armed for an argument with both facts and indignation (US). L19–M20.

Beard. An American with a muffled enunciation. E20.

Beast. A bicycle. L19.

Beat. 'A naval seaman's lady friend' (Bowen). L19–E20. *Beat the booby.* Warm oneself by slapping one's hands against one's sides. 19.

Beau-trap. 'A loose stone in a pavement, under which water lodges, and on being trod upon, squirts it up, to the great damage of white stockings' (Grose). L18–E19.

Beaver. A late lunch. L17.

Bed. Bed-filling. A period of horizontal repose after dinner to aid digestion. L19–E20. *Bed-tick.* A British sailors' derogatory term for the Stars and Stripes. M19–E20. *Bruise the bed.* Foul one's sleeping place (from *brewes*: oatmeal and salt beef boiled together). L18–E19.

Bedford go. 'A peculiar oily chuckle' (Ware). M19.

Beef. Beef a bravo. Whip up applause in a music hall. L19. *Be in a man's beef.* Stab him with a sword. L18–E19. *Be in a woman's beef.* Have sexual intercourse with her. L18–M19. *On the beefment.* Vigilant. L19.

Beer-lever. An aeroplane joystick (WWII). M20.

Beetle. Beetle-bait. Australian treacle (WWI). E20.

Beggar. Beggar boy's ass. Money. L19–E20. *Beggar's plush.* Corduroy. L17–18. *Beggars' velvet.* 'Downy particles which accumulate under furniture from the negligence of housemaids. Otherwise called "sluts'-wool" ' (Hotten). 19–E20.

Belinda. A barrage balloon (WWII). M20.

Beller-croaker. Radiantly lovely. M–L19.

Belly. Belly cheat. 1. An apron. E17–E19. 2. A false bump employed by women wishing to appear pregnant. 19. *Belly-go-firster.* A pre-emptive punch to the stomach, intended to finish a fight before it begins. 19.

Bender. 1. A sixpence. L18–E20. 2. A stroke of the cane applied to a bent-over schoolboy. L19.

Bene darkmans. Goodnight. M16–L18.

Benny, have a. Unwittingly wet one's bed. L19–E20.

Berkeleys. A woman's breasts. L19.

Bernice. Powdered cocaine, for snorting (US). E–M20.

Bethlehemite. A Christmas carol-singer. L18–E19.

Betty. 1. A husband who does his fair share of domestic chores. 19–M20. 2. Potter about. M19–E20.

Betwattled. Dumbfounded. L18–E19.

Bexandebs. A collective term for pleasant young Jewish women. L18–E20.

Bible. The large axe carried by a boatswain. L18–M19. *Bible class.* A brawl. L19.

Bidgee. A methylated-spirits cocktail from Australia. Mix equal quantities of meths and cheap wine (preferably white); stir in a tablespoon of shoe polish, a smattering of raisins, a smidgeon of sugar, and a *soupçon* of water; for extra piquancy add tobacco to taste; no ice; serve. E–M20.

Biffin. A close companion. M–L19.

Bilbo. A fine or large sword. L17–18.

Billy noodle. A man who believes himself irresistible to women (US). 19.

Bimbo. 1. A tough guy (US). E20. 2. A young American woman with a wayward moral compass. E–M20. 3. A tramp's compadre. E–M20.

Bindle stiff. An American itinerant who carries his blanket in a roll. L19–M20.

Binge. 'A high degree of physical and mental fitness' (*Forces' Slang*) (WWII). M20.

Bingo boy. A loutish brandy-drinker. L17–E19.

Bing room. A drug den, or shooting gallery (US). M20.

Binting. Go to Cairo in search of women (WWI). E20.

Birmingham-conscience. 'Very bad' (B.E.).

Bishop. 1. A voluminous condom. L18–E19. 2. A chamberpot. 19–E20. 3. Murder by drowning. M–L19. See also *Shoot a bishop.*

Biskiwits. Prisoners of war (WWI). E20.

Bismarcker. Cheat, especially at billiards or cards. L19.

Bit. Bit of pooh. Smooth talk. L19–E20. *Bit of prairie.* 'A momentary lull in the traffic at any point in the Strand' (Ware). M19–E20. *Bits of grey.* 'Elderly victims of both sexes present at balls and marriages, especially the latter, to give an air of staid dignity' (Ware). L19.

Bitch. Go whoring. M17–M19. *Bitches' heaven.* Boston, Mass. (once famous for the number of its cheap prostitutes). E20. *Bitches' wine.* Champagne. M–L19. *Stand bitch.* Make or serve tea. L18–E19. See also *Son of a bitch.*

Bite the roger. Steal a suitcase. L17–E19.

Black. Black arse. A kettle or pot. L17–E19. *Black-bottle scene.* The practice of hurling beer bottles at obnoxious individuals. E–M19. *Black hand gang.* A body of soldiers selected for a dangerous task (WWI). E20. *Black Hole.* Cheltenham (from the number of retired India hands living there). L19. *Black Monday.* The first Monday of term, when schoolboys have to hand in their holiday homework. M18–E19. *Black mummer.* An actor with filthy personal habits. 19. *Black neb.* A radical democrat, especially one supportive of the French Revolution. L18. *Black-outs.* The regulation underwear of female personnel in the armed forces (WWII). M20. *Black-silk barges.* 'Stout women who ought to avoid dances. They dress in black silk to moderate in appearance their amplitude' (Ware). L19–E20. *Black spice racket.* The business of stealing the soot from chimney-sweepers. 18–E19. *Blush like a black dog.* Be utterly without shame. M16–18.

Bladder of lard. A derogatory term for a bald man; a slap-head. M–L19. See also *Quiff the bladder.*

Blanket drill. An afternoon snooze (WWI). L19–E20.

Bleating cheat. A sheep. 17–E19.

Blow one's screw. Squander one's salary. M–L19.

Blighty bag. The bag used to hold a wounded soldier's possessions (WWI). E20.

Blind. Blind Cupid. The posterior. E–M19. *Blind hookey system.* Reckless gambling. M–L19. *Blind man's holiday.* Night time. L16–L19.

Blink-fencer. A spectacle-seller. M19–E20.

Blitz buggy. An ambulance (WWII). M20.

Bloated aristocrat. 'A street term for any decently dressed person' (Hotten). M18–L19.

Blob. A glass of beer (WWI). E20.

Blood and thunder. An invigorating mixture of port and brandy. E–M19.

9

Blow the grounsils. Have sex on the stairs or the floor. 17–18.

Blowsabella. A woman with dishevelled hair. 18–E19.

Blubber hunter. A whaling ship. M19–E20.

Bludger. A petty thief with an aptitude for violence. M–L19.

Blue. Blue bottle. A policeman. M–L19. *Blue devils.* 'Horrification' (Bee). L18–M20. *Blue flier.* A fast kangaroo (AUS). 19–M20. *Blue goose.* A general holding cell (US). E20. *Blue Monday.* An illicit extension of the weekend. L19–E20. *Blue nose.* A Canadian, especially one from Nova Scotia. M–L19. *Blue pig.* American 'whiskey'. E–M20. *Blue pigeon.* Someone who steals the lead from roofs. M18–19. *Blue ruin.* Gin. 19. (Also *Blue ribbon, Blue stone, Blue tape, Light blue.*) *Blues.* 'Variously defined as a form of jazz, feigned gaiety, camouflaged joy, and an easy-going heart disease' (Weseen) (US). M19–20.

Blunk. A squall of unpleasant weather. L18–E19.

Blurbisher. A publisher prone to promoting his wares with extravagant blurbs (US). E–M20.

Boarding school. 'Bridewell, Newgate, or any other prison or house of correction' (Grose). L17–M19.

Bob. 1. A shoplifter's assistant, or recipient of stolen goods. L17–19. 2. Gin. 18. (Also *Royal bob.*) *Bob tail.* 1. A lewd woman. 17–18. 2. An impotent man. 17–18. 3. A partridge. L18–E19. *Dry bob.* 1. A witty riposte. 17–18. 2. Copulation without ejaculation. M18–19. 3. A public-schoolboy cricketer. 19–20. *Go-along bob.* A sheep-drover with a reputation. E19. See also *Shiny Bob.*

Body snatcher. 1. A cat-stealer. M–L19. 2. A cab driver. M19. 3. A stretcher-bearer (WWI). E20.

Boette. A hobo of the feminine persuasion (US). E–M20.

Boffo. The sum of $1 (US). E–M20.

Bogie hole. A swimming hole, or bath (AUS). L19–M20.

Bohemian bungery. A 'public-house patronised by struggling authors' (Ware). L19.

Boil one's lobster. Resign from the clergy to become a soldier. M18–E19.

Bolly dog. A policeman. E18.

Bolo. A spy (wwi). E20.

Bombardier Fritz. Chips (*pommes de terre frites*) (wwi). E20.

Bombay oyster. Milk with a double shot of castor oil. 19–E20.

Bone. Bone picker. A footman (because he is frequently fed on left-overs). L18–19. *Bone-yard aggregation.* An American baseball team composed of has-beens and no-hopers. E–M20.

Bong. 1. Get the joke long after everyone else (us). E–M20. 2. Be dead (aus). 19–M20.

Bongo Boosh. A delicious morsel of food (wwi). E20.

Bonk. 1. A small, steep hill. M–L19. 2. Bombard (wwi). E20.

Bonnet. Provide an alibi, or otherwise corroborate a false statement. L18–M19.

Booboisie. The dumb and gullible – 'often used to mean the great mass of average Americans' (Weseen). E20.

Boodle. Money earned through bribery, fraud, or scam. M19–20. See also *Fake boodle.*

Boofhead. An extreme idiot (aus). 19–M20.

Booka. Hungry (Anglo-Indian). L19–E20.

Boomer. An itinerant worker in North America. L19–M20.

Boop. Make a mountain out of a molehill (wwii). M20.

Bosh. 1. A violin. M–L19. 2. A butter substitute. L19–E20.

Bosky. Mildly tipsy. M18–M19.

Bosom friends. Lice. 18–E20.

Boss. 1. A large woman. L16–M17. 2. A myopic individual. M19–E20. *Bossers.* A pair of spectacles. L19–E20. *Boss windjammer.* The leader of an American circus band. E20.

Bossy in a bowl. American beef stew. E20.

Bostruchyzer. A small comb used for curling a male undergraduate's whiskers. L19.

Bottle. Bottle the tot. Illicitly store up one's daily rum ration in expectation of some special occasion (wwii). M20. *On the bottle.* Working as a rent boy. E–M20.

Botty. Swaggeringly conceited. M–L19.

Boughs, be wide in the. Possess ample hips and a large posterior. E–M19.

Bounce. 1. Cherry brandy. L19–E20. 2. An enormous dogfish. L19–E20. *Bouncer.* 1. A fat person. L18–E19. 2. A shoplifter who engages a shopkeeper in conversation while he pilfers his store. M19. *Bouncing ben.* An intellectual. M–L19. *Bouncing cheat.* A bottle. E18–M19.

Boung nipper. A cutpurse. M17–L19.

Bow-wow. A derogatory name for a native of Boston, Mass. L18–E19. *Bow-wow mutton.* Dog meat. L18–L19.

Bowyangs. The strings tied below the knees of a workman's trousers to keep them out of the dirt (AUS). 19–M20.

Box. Box harry. Eat tea and dinner together in one meal. M19. *Box the Jesuit and get cockroaches.* A term for masturbation favoured by seamen. M18–19.

Bozzimacoo. Kiss my arse, as said in Yorkshire. M19–E20.

Brace up. 'Dispose of stolen goods by pledging them for the utmost you can get at a pawnbroker's' (Egan). E19–E20.

Bradshaw. A person with a head for figures (from the famed railway guide). L19–E20.

Bramble-gelder. A farmer or agricultural labourer. M19–E20.

Bread, in bad. In a disagreeable predicament. M18–M19.

Breath strong enough to carry coal. Noxiously drunk. L19–E20.

Brian. Gin. M–L19. (Also *Brian O'Lynn.*)

Brick. 'About the highest compliment that in one word can be paid one man. Said to be derived from an expression of Aristotle's – *tetragonos aner* [a four-square man]' (Hotten). M19–E20. *Make brick walls.* Consume one's food without observing the niceties of mastication. L19–E20. *Brick-layer.* A cleric. M–L19.

Bridget. Obtain money from maidservants under false pretences. M–L19.

Brilliant. Raw gin. E–M19. (Also *Brilliant stark-naked.*)

Brim. 1. An abandoned woman. L17–M19. 2. An aggressive one. L18–19.

Bristol. Bristol man. 'The son of an Irish thief and a Welsh whore' (*Lex.Bal.*). E–M19. *Bristol milk.* Sherry (according to some, from its popularity in the city as a morning tipple). M17–E19.

Bristol stone. A fake diamond. 17–18.

Brits up, have the. Be scared (AUS). E–M20.

Broganeer. The owner of a strong Irish accent. L18–E19.

Broken brigade. 'Poor, younger sons living on their wits' (Ware). L19.

Brolly hop. A parachute jump (WWII). M20.

Brother. Brother of the gusset. A pimp. L17–19. *Brother starling.* 'One who lies with the same woman, that is, builds in the same nest' (Grose). L17–E19.

Brown. Brownie. 1. A polar bear. M19–E20. 2. A cheap cigarette. L19–E20. *Brown Janet.* A knapsack. L18–E20. *Brown-out Romeo.* An Australian who takes advantage of bad street-lighting to pester women. L19–M20.

Brutal brodie. A failure (US). E–M20.

Buck. 1. 'A blind horse, also a gay debauchee' (Grose). L18–E19. 2. An unlicensed taxi-driver. M19–E20.

Buckie. Any tailor or cobbler not respected by his peers. L19–E20.

Budge. Sneaking budge. One who slips into houses under the cover of darkness to steal clothes. M17–E19.

Budgeree. Good (AUS, from Aborigine). L18–E20.

Buff. A female student at an American university. E20.

Buffer. 1. A dog. M16–M19. 2. A dog-stealer or horse thief who takes animals for their skins. L17–18. 3. An oath-taker willing to stand bail fraudulently for a criminal. 19.

Buffy. Inebriated. M19–E20.

Bug. 1. 'A nickname given by the Irish to Englishmen; bugs having (as it is said) been introduced into Ireland by the English' (Grose). M18–19. 2. Replace expensive materials with cheaper ones when making a hat. L18–E19.

Bugaboo. A debt collector. 19.

Bugger. One who purloins breast-pins from drunks. 19.

Buggy bandit. An American car thief; a joy-rider. E–M20.

Bulkateer. An American who values quantity over quality. 20.

Bull. 1. Hair extensions for women. L17–M18. 2. A broken-winded horse. L19–E20. *Bull buster.* 'One with a morbid passion for assaulting the police' (Irwin) (US). E–M20. *Bull chin.* A podgy child, or chubber. L17–E19. *Bull dogs.* Pistols. L17–19. *Bull the cask.* 'Pour hot water into an empty rum puncheon, and let it stand until it extracts the spirit from the wood. The mixture is drunk by sailors in default of something stronger' (Hotten). E–M19. *Bull's aunts.* A pair of trousers (US). E–M20.

Bully-rock. A boon companion. L16–E18.

Bum. Bum-brusher. A schoolmaster. E18–M19. *Bum factory.* A lodging house or hostel for itinerants (US). E–M20. *Bummer.* A layabout or loafer. M–L19.

Bumble dog. An unthinking card-player (US). M20.

Bumf. Lavatory paper (from *Bum fodder*). L19–20. Hence, routine paperwork and orders (WWI). E20.

Bummaree. An unlicensed and unscrupulous speculator in fish. L18–L19.

Bumper. 'A full glass; in all likelihood from its convexity or bump at the top; some derive it from a full glass formerly drank to the health of the pope—*au bon père*' (*Lex.Bal.*). M17–E19.

Bun. Bun-duster. A man who 'frequents teas' (US). E–M20. *Bun-strangler.* A military teetotaller. L19–E20. *Bun-worry.* A ladies' tea-party attended by sailors. L19–E20.

Bungdung. A noisy firework (AUS). 19–M20.

Bung it in. Gin. E–M20.

Bungler. 'An unperforming husband' (B.E.). 17–18.

Bunker shy. 'Afraid of being forced into unnatural sexual relations' (Irwin) (US). E–M20.

Bunter. 'A low dirty prostitute, half whore and half beggar' (Grose). E18–L19. *Bunter's tea.* Gin. M18.

Bunty. A short soldier. L19–E20.

Bunyip. An outrageously sly impostor (AUS). M19–E20.

Burke. 1. Murder stealthily, usually by throttling. M19. 2. Suppress a book before publication; stifle a project. M–L19. 3. Dye one's moustaches. M19.

Burning the water. Nocturnal salmon-spearing. 19.

Burster and beeswax. An undersized cheese roll. M–L19.

Bushel bubby. A well-endowed woman. M18–19.

Bushing party. A picnic in Australia. 19–M20.

Busk. 1. Embark upon a piratical cruise. 18–E20. 2. Hawk pornographic literature and songs in public houses. M19.

Bus napper. A constable. L18–E19.

Buss beggar. 'An old superannuated fumbler, whom none but beggars will suffer to kiss them' (Grose). 18–E19.

Bustle. Money. E–M19.

Butch. The owner of a small confectionery concession. E20.

Butter. Buttered bun. 'Lying with a woman that has been just lain with by another man' (B.E.). L17–E20. *Butter upon bacon.* Too much of a good thing. L19.

Buxton bloater. A man or woman so obese they have to be wheeled in a bath-chair. L19–E20.

Buzz. 'Share equally the last of a bottle of wine, when there is not enough for a full glass' (Hotten). 19. *Buzza.* Challenge someone to drink a bottle's remains in one go. L18–E19.

Byng boys. Canadian soldiers (WWI). E20.

Cab. Cab joint. A brothel which gains its business via taxi-drivers (US). M20. *Cab moll.* A prostitute with a professional penchant for public transport. M19–E20.

Cabbage. Cloth stolen by a tailor from his employer. M17–M19.

Cable hanger. An illicit oyster-hunter. E18–E20.

Cackling fart. An egg. L17–18.

Cad. Cad-catcher. A work of art deliberately created to appeal to those with more money than taste. 19. *Cad-mad.* 'The vainglory and superciliousness which overcome, and permanently, the better sense of *nouveaux riches*' (Ware). L19. *Cads on castors.* Cyclists. L19.

Cafishio. An Argentinian white-slaver with a side-line in pimping. E20.

Cakey-pannum-fencer. 'A man who sells street pastry' (Hotten). 19.

Calathumpian. The devotee of a made-up religion. M20.

Calf slobbers. A cowboy's name for a meringue (US). M20.

California. California blanket. A newspaper used as bedding in America. E–M20. *Californian.* A dried kipper. M–L19.

Calorific mamma. A young woman with powerful sex appeal, a 'hotty' (US). E–M20.

Camac. Anything more complicated or expensive than it needs to be. 19.

Cam-a-lankee. Green peas. E–M19.

Camel. In South Africa, a giraffe. L19–E20. *Camel punk.* A juvenile camel-attendant (US). E20. *Camel's complaint.* Depression, i.e. having the hump. L19.

Camera obscura. The posterior (US). L19–E20.

Cane. Shell relentlessly (WW1). E20.

Caniculars. Appalling poetry; doggerel. L19.

Can I help you with that? A phrase used to proposition a woman. L19–E20.

Canned willie. Tinned corned beef for sailors (US). L19–E20.

Canniken. The plague. L17–E19.

Canoeuvre. 'A low manoeuvre or essay at deception' (Bee). E–M19.

Cant or *Canting.* 'A kind of gibberish used by thieves and gypsies, called likewise Pedlar's French, the slang, etc.' (Grose). 17–19. *Canting crew.* Criminals and vagabonds distinguished by their peculiar mode of expression. 17–19.

Canterbury tale. An immensely tedious story. M16–E19.

Cape Horn fever. The practice of malingering in a sailing ship during stormy weather. M19–E20.

Captain. Captain Bow-wow. 'A famous old-time Clyde passenger skipper who, coming alongside and suddenly seeing there was no fender out, seized a passenger's dog by the tail and used him' (Bowen). L19–E20. *Captain Cook.* A wild or shabby-looking New Zealand pig (AUS, NZ). L19–20. *Captain Macfluffer.* Forget one's lines. L19–E20. *Captain Queernabs.* 'A shabby ill-dressed fellow' (Grose). L17–E19.

Capture the pickled biscuit. Win first prize; come up trumps (AUS). L19–20.

Caravanserai. A railway station. M–L19.

Carpet-slipper bastard. A heavy shell passing almost silently high overhead (WW1). E20.

Carrion. Ship's food. L19–E20. *Carrion-hunter.* An undertaker. L18–M19.

Carriwitchet. 'A hoaxing, puzzling question, not admitting of a satisfactory answer, as … "If a bushel of apples cost ten shillings, how long will it take for an oyster to eat its way through a barrel of soap?" ' (Hotten). L19.

Casabianca. The last cigarette in the packet. M19–E20.

Cat. Cat and kitten hunt. The business of stealing pewter pots from public-houses. E–M19. *Cat lap.* Tea. L17–19. *Cat match.* A game of bowls featuring a hustler. L17–18. *Cat's meat.* The lungs. Usually applied to a consumptive, e.g. his *cat's meat* is bad. L18–E19. *Cat-stabber.* A soldier's clasp-knife (WWI). E20. *Cat's water.* Gin. M19–E20. *Pinch the cat.* Meditatively fondle one's genitalia through one's trouser pocket. L19–20. See also *Shoot the cat; Singed cat.*

Catamaran. 'An old scraggy woman; from a kind of float made of spars and yards lashed together, for saving ship-wrecked persons' (Grose).

Catawampously. Vigorously, with enthusiasm. M19–E20.

Caterwaul. Go out at night in search of amorous adventure. L16–E20.

Cathedral. Old-fashioned, out of date. L17–E19.

Cauliflower. 1. A large white wig, as worn by distinguished clergymen. E18. 2. A woman's private parts. 18–19. 3. The foaming head on a pint of beer. 19.

Cawsy. A lavatory (from 'causeway', i.e. the street). 19–E20.

Caz. Cheese. 19. *As good as caz.* A certainty. 19.

Celestial poultry. Angels. M19–E20.

Cellar flap. 1. A noisy shuffling dance popular with coster-mongers. M–L19.

CGI (Corticene-grabber's itch). The overwhelming desire when being dive-bombed to hurl oneself on the deck (AUS: WWII). M20.

Chalk. Slash an unsuspecting passer-by across the face with a knife for fun. 18–19.

Chamber of horrors. 1. The peeresses' gallery in the House of Lords. M–L19. 2. A sausage. L19.

Chameleon diet. A starvation diet. L17–18.

Character academy. An illicit business providing false references for otherwise unemployable servants. M19.

Chariot-buzzing. Pocket-picking while on a bus. M–L19.

Charley horse. Sudden cramp in an arm or leg (US). L19–M20.

Chatts. 1. The gallows. M16–18. 2. Lice. 'Perhaps an abbreviation of chattels, lice being the chief live stock or chattels ... of the canting crew' (Grose). L17–E20. *Chatty dosser.* A filthy down-and-out. M–L19.

Cheaters. Close-fitting, well-elasticated underpants for men. E20.

Cheese. Cheese and crust. Jesus Christ! L19–E20. *Cheese-toaster.* A sword. M18–E20. *The cheese.* 1. The done thing; the fashion. 19. 2. One's wife (AUS). E–M20. See also *Howling cheese*; *Mouse in a cheese, speak like a.*

Cherry. Cherry-coloured cat. A black cat (there are black cherries as well as red ones). L18–E19. *Cherry-merry.* A gift of money. M–L19. *Cherry-merry-bamboo.* A beating. M–L19. *Go to the cherries.* Go dog-racing. E–M20.

Cherubims. 'Peevish children, because cherubims and seraphims continually do cry' (Grose). L18–E19.

Chew a lone nabisco. Attend a party at which one knows nobody (US). E–M20.

Chicagorilla. An American enforcer or gunman. E20.

Chicken. Chicken-breasted. A term used to describe a flat-chested woman. L18–E19. *Chicken nabob.* A diminutive nabob, i.e. 'one returned from the East Indies with but a moderate fortune of fifty or sixty thousand pounds' (*Lex.Bal.*). L18–E19.

Chinafication. 'The reduction of a country to a state of helplessness' (Weseen) (US). E–M20.

Chinese. Chinese attack. A feint (WWI). E20. *Chinese compliment.* Insincere agreement with another's opinion when one has already made up one's mind. L19–E20.

Chinkers. Handcuffs joined together by a chain. 19–E20.

Chin-wag. 'Officious impertinence' (Hotten). M–L19.

Chirper. One of a gang extorting money from music-hall artistes by fear of turning the audience against them so that they are booed off the stage. L19–E20.

Chittiface. 'A little puny child' (B.E.). L17–19.

Chivalry. Sexual intercourse. L18–L19.

Choking pie. A trick played on someone who falls asleep in public. Cotton wrapped in a tube of paper is set alight and the smoke directed up the victim's nostrils. M17–M19.

Chonkey. A dubious meat pie. M–L19.

Chooch hat. A particularly dapper item of headgear, often worn for poodle-faking (q.v.) (wwii). M20.

Chop up the whiners. Rush through one's prayers. L17–M19.

Christened by twelve godfathers. Tried before a jury (and found guilty). M19.

Christian. A tradesman offering credit (he 'has faith'). E–M19. *Christian pony.* A sedan-chair carrier. L18–E19.

Chuck. Chuck a dummy. Pretend to be ill in order to gain sympathy (us). E–M20. *Chuck a jolly.* Heartily promote something wrong. M–L19.

Chuckaroo. A boy who runs errands for soldiers. L19.

Chuckle-head. An individual who habitually eats himself into a stupor; a wobble-chops. E19.

Chummage. The money paid by a rich prisoner to cell-mates in order to get the room to himself. M18–19.

Chummy flyabout. A privately owned small aircraft (us). M20.

Church. Churchwarden. 1. A Sussex term for a cormorant or shag. L18–E19. 2. A long clay pipe. M–L19. *Churchyard luck.* In a large but poor family, the death of a child, i.e. one less mouth to feed. 19–E20.

Cinder. Cinder-garbler. A maidservant. L18–19. *Cinder-sifter.* 1. A fashionable woman's hat with an open-work brim. L19–E20. 2. A tramp on the railways (us). E–M20.

Cinemaelstrom. The perpetual cash-flow crises of a moving-picture mogul (us). E–M20.

Circumbendibus. A roundabout route or tale. L17–M19.

Circus. A live sex show (clowns optional). 19–M20.

City light horse. A secretary sleeping with her boss. M20.

Clank napper. A silver-tankard thief (Grose, 1823).

Clapperdogeon. A beggar born and bred. M16–19.

Classifist. 'A person who is a pacifist as regards international war but who indulges in or supports class war' (Weseen) (US). E–M20.

Claws for breakfast. A flogging with a cat-o'-nine-tails. M19.

Clean potato. An Australian without a criminal past. 19.

Clear crystal. Gin; also other spirits. M–L19.

Cleymes. 'Artificial sores, made by beggars to excite charity' (Grose). M17–M19.

Clip-up. The 'schoolboys' method of casting lots by approaching each other … with a heel-to-toe step. He who finds that the last gap is too small for the length of his foot is the loser' (Partridge). L19–20.

Cloak-twitcher. One who hangs round dark alleyways with the aim of snatching cloaks from passers-by. E18–E20.

Cloddy. Distinguished-looking (of a person or animal). L19.

Cloflumpux. The sound made by a falling body when it hits the ground (US). M19.

Clouting. The business of picking pockets for handkerchiefs. L18–M19.

Cloven. 'A woman who passes for a maid, but is not one' (Grose). L18–E19.

Club and stick. A detective, i.e. a 'dick' (US). M20.

Clunch. A clumsy buffoon. L18–E19.

Coax. Conceal the dirty or torn part of one's stockings in one's shoes. M18–E19.

Cobbler. The worst sheep in a flock (AUS). L19–20.

Cock. Cock ale. 'A provocative drink' (Grose). *Cock-and-breeches.* A stout little boy. M19. *Cock-chafer.* A prison treadmill. M–L19. *Cock my cap.* Gin. M18.

Cockatoo. A small Antipodean farmer. M19–E20.

Cocktails, the. Diarrhoea (AUS). L19–20.

Cod-bangers. 'Gorgeously arrayed sailors' (Ware). L19–E20.

Cods. 1. The scrotum. 16–E20. 2. A curate. M18–E19.

Coffee. Coffee royal. The day's first mug of coffee on board a sailing ship. L19–E20. *Coffee-shop.* A water closet. L18–20. *Make a coffee-house of a woman's* ——. Fail to reach orgasm, i.e. 'go in and out and spend nothing' (Grose). L18–E19.

Cogman. A beggar pretending to be a shipwrecked sailor. 19.

Cold. Cold blood. An off-licence. M–L19. *Cold burning.* An informal punishment administered by soldiers to one of their group, in which a bottle of cold water is poured slowly down the upraised sleeve of the victim until it dribbles out of the bottom of his breeches. M18–E19. *Cold cream.* Gin. M–L19.

Collah carriage. A railway coach filled with women. L19.

Collie shangle. A sharp quarrel. L19–E20.

Colt. A hirer of horses to highwaymen. L17–E19.

Columbus circle. A bag beneath an actor's eye (US). E–M20.

Come. Come the acid. Attempt to borrow money from a fellow soldier (the ultimate test of friendship). E20. *Come the bag.* Irritate everyone in the vicinity (WWI). E20. *Come the Traviata.* Pretend to be consumptive, and so appear pale and interesting. M19.

Comfort. Gin. M18. *Comfortable importance.* A wife. L17–20.

Comic Cuts. Information provided by military intelligence; divisional orders (WWI). E20.

Commodity. 'The private parts of a modest woman, and the public parts of a prostitute' (Grose). L16–19.

Compo king. 'A social parasite who makes a practice of injuring himself or malingering in order to secure workers' compensation' (Baker, NZ). M20.

Comstockism. 'Opposition to the nude in art' (US). L19–E20.

Concertina. A wrinkled sheep (AUS). L19–20.

Congo patter. Slang in Liverpool. L19.

Conish cove. A gentleman, in Scots cant. E–M19.

Conk. An informer, or grass. E–M19.

Conscience keeper. 'A superior, who by his influence, makes his dependents act as he pleases' (*Lex.Bal.*). L18–M19.

Constant screamer. A concertina. M19–E20.

Constitutional. Gin and bitters (AUS). L19–20.

Consumer. A butler. E18–L19.

Content. Gingerbread dissolved in milk as an alternative to drinking chocolate. L18–E19.

Continual round of pleasure. A tramp's existence (US). E20.

Convenient. A mistress or prostitute. M17–E19.

Cony. Cony-catcher. A trickster, or con artist. L16–M19. *Cony-wabble.* A dupe, or mark. 18.

Cooch. The Turkish 'muscle dance' (US). E–M20.

Cookie. An American with a cocaine habit. E20. *Cookie pusher.* An ineffectual student lothario (US). M20. *Cookie-shine.* A tea-party. M–L19.

Cooler. The backside – 'it is principally used to signify a woman's posteriors' (*Lex.Bal.*). E19.

Cooter-goosht. Revolting food. L19–E20.

Cootie cage. A bunk in an American logging camp. E–M20.

Copper-tail. A representative of the lower classes (AUS). L19.

Core. Shop-lift items of small value. E–M19.

Cork. 1. A Scots small-businessman or foreman. M–L19. 2. A bankrupt. L19.

Corporal and four, mount a. 'Be guilty of onanism: the thumb is the corporal, the four fingers the privates' (Grose). L18–E20.

Corporation, glorious. A superlatively large belly. M18–19.

Corpse worship. 'The extreme use of flowers at funerals' which originated with Queen Victoria (Ware). L19–E20.

Corrobberee. 'A drunken spree, in which there is much yelling' (Ware). L19–E20.

Corybungus. A boxer's backside. M–L19.

Cot(quean). Quot. A domesticated man; one 'who meddles with woman's household business, particularly in the kitchen' (*Lex.Bal.*). L17–E19.

Cotton-top. A woman whose respectable appearance belies her unrespectable behaviour. M–L19.

Couch a porker. Go to sleep. 18.

Cousin Betty. A woman not over-endowed with intelligence. M19–E20. The male equivalent is a *Cousin Tom.*

Cover-slut. An apron. 17–19.

Cow-spanker. An Antipodean dairy farmer or cattle-banger. 19–20.

Coxey. A firebrand political leader. L19.

Crack. 1. A prostitute. M17–E19. 2. Well-dried firewood. M19. *Crack a boo.* Give in to one's emotions, or reveal a secret (AUS). 19–20. *Crack a Judy's tea-cup.* Relieve a woman of her virginity. 19–E20. *Crack-fencer.* A purveyor of nuts. M–L19.

Cramp. Cramp dodge. Pretended writers' cramp (a schoolboy ailment). L19. *Cramp words.* The death sentence. 18–E19.

Crank. 1. Epilepsy (the 'falling sickness') M16–18. 2. Gin and water. L18–M19. *Cranky gowk.* An awkward teenager (US). L19–E20.

Crap. 1. Money. L17–19. 2. The gallows. L18–19. 3. Mixed-up printer's type (i.e. 'pie'). M–L19.

Crashing cheats. 1. Teeth. M16–M19. 2. Fruit. M16–E17.

Crawler. A docile, contented cow (NZ). 19–20.

Cream of the valley. Gin. M19. (Also *Cream of the wilderness.*)

Creature. Gin, or any other spiritous liquor. L17–18.

Credentials. A man's genitals. L19–20.

Creeping barrage. A name given to the weakest convalescing soldiers, from the slowness of their marching (WWI). E20.

Croakumshire. 'Northumberland, from the particular croaking in the pronunciation of the people of that county, especially about Newcastle and Morpeth' (Grose). 18–19.

Crocus. A surgeon or doctor of limited abilities. L18–19.

Cronk. A nobbled racehorse (AUS). L19.

Crony. A Scotsman's potato. 19–20.

Croppie. 'One who has had his hair cut in prison' (Ducange), i.e. an ex-con. M–L19.

Cross-bite. The entrapment and blackmail of a man by a husband and (pretended) wife. L18–19.

Crummy-lass. A term of approbation for a big girl. E–M19.

Crump. A supplier of false witnesses to a solicitor. L17–E19.

Crumpet-face. An individual whose complexion has been scarred by smallpox. M19–E20.

Crusoe. A labourer in, or owner of, an ironworks. L19–E20.

Crusty beau. The sort of man who uses too much make-up and not enough cleanser. L17–E19.

Cry pork. Tip off an undertaker about a prospective customer. L18–M19.

Cucumber. A tailor. L17–E19.

Cuddy. An affectionate name for a donkey. E18–19. *Cuddy-jig.* The undignified movements of a landlubber attempting to keep his balance on board ship. M19–20. *Cuddy-leg.* A colossal herring. L19–20.

Cuerpo, in. Naked, in the buff. 18.

Cuffer. A lie, or highly improbable story. M–L19.

Culch. Scraps and off-cuts of poor-quality meat. L–M19.

Cull's content. The man is past complaining – said of one murdered while attempting to fight off robbers. L18–E19.

Culty-gun. The penis. 19.

Cunning man. 'A cheat, who pretends by his skill in astrology to assist persons in recovering stolen goods' (*Lex.Bal.*). L18–M19.

Cupboard-headed. 'One whose head is both wooden and hollow' (Hotten). M–L19.

Cupid's kettle drums. A woman's breasts. L18–E19.

Curate. 1. The thinly buttered top half of a toasted muffin. 19. 2. A used handkerchief (not one kept for show). L19–20. *Curate's delight.* A multi-level cake-stand (ideally fully laden). L19–M20.

Curl. Curled darlings. 'A name given to military officers immediately after the Crimean War, which once more brought soldiers into fashion. Referred to the waving of the long beard and sweeping moustache' (Ware). M–L19. *Curls.* 'Human teeth obtained by the body-snatchers' (Bee). E–M19.

Curtail. 1. A thief in a short jacket. 16–17. 2. A thief who cuts off pieces of cloth hanging out of shop windows or from women's dresses. 18.

Cushion. Cushion-cuffer. An especially vigorous preacher. L17–M18. *Deserve the cushion.* 'A saying of one whose wife is brought to bed of a boy, implying that having done his business effectually, he may now indulge or repose himself' (Grose). M17–E19.

Cut. Cut a bosh. Stand out from the crowd. M18–E19. *Cut didoes.* Lark about. M19–E20. *Cut mugs.* Pull faces or gurn in a humorous manner. 19. *Cut queer whiddes.* Swear. M16–E19. *Cuts.* A sailor who regards himself as a bit of a wit. L19–20. *Cut sublime.* Ignore the presence of someone in Cambridge by pretending to admire King's College Chapel. L18–E19. *Cut up well.* 1. Die rich. L18–E19. 2. Look good naked. M–L19.

Cuthbert. A fit man exempted from military service because a civil servant; a shirker more generally (WWI). E20.

Cutty-gun. A stubby pipe favoured by Scots seafarers. On no account to be mistaken for a culty-gun (q.v.). M19–E20.

Cycling fringes. 'Especially prepared forehead-hair to be worn by such women bikers as had not abjured all feminine vanities' (Ware). L19–E20.

Cyclophobist. 1. An individual with a phobia of junk mail. L19. 2. A right-minded despiser of cyclists. L19–E20.

Dab it up. Agree to cohabit with a woman. E–M19.

Daffy. Daffy's elixir. Gin. E–M19. *Daffy it.* Drink gin. M19.

Daisy-picker. A chaperone. L19–E20.

Damme-boy. 'A roaring mad, blustering fellow, a scourer of the streets' (B.E.). M17–E18.

Damned good swine up. An enjoyably vigorous disagreement. L19.

Dance. Dance barefoot. Said of a woman whose younger sister marries first. L16–L18. *Dance upon nothing.* Be hanged. 19–20.

Dando. A voracious eater, especially one with a habit of bilking restaurants. M–L19.

Dandy. Dandy horse. A velocipede. E–M19. *Dandypratt.* An absolute nonentity. 16–19.

Danna-drag. A night-soil cart. 19.

Darby roll. The peculiar gait of a shackled prisoner. 19.

Dark. Dark cully. 'A married man that keeps a mistress, whom he visits only at night' (Grose). 18–E19. *Dark horse.* The other participant in a blind date (US). E20.

Davy Jones. Davy Jones's natural children. Pirates and smugglers. 19. *Davy Jones's shocker.* A depth charge (WWII). M20.

27

Dead. Dead man. A baker. M19. *Dead man's effects.* False teeth (wwii). M20. *Dead rabbit.* Anything worthless or unwanted (us). M20. *Dead-room chiseler.* A mourner for hire (us). E20. *Deadly nevergreen.* The gallows. L18–E19. *Deady.* Gin. E–M19. (Also *Dead eye.*)

Deboswellize. Debunk someone's reputation (us). E20.

Decencies. 'Pads used by actors, as distinct from actresses, to ameliorate outline' (Ware). L19–E20.

Dedigitate. Pull one's finger out (wwii). M20.

Dee donk. A soldiers' name for a Frenchman. M19. (The French reciprocated in kind by referring to the British as 'I says'; and similarly, nowadays, as 'les fuckoffs'.)

Demi. Demi-hag. A long-barrelled, heavy-bore, muzzle-loading pistol. 19. *Demi-rep.* 'A woman of doubtful character' (Grose). M18–19.

Demublican. An American swing-voter. E20.

Dennis. A lightweight walking stick. M–L19.

Devil. 1. Coloured thread woven into naval ropes, cables or sails in an attempt to prevent dockyard thefts. L18–E19. 2. Gin infused with chillies. E–M19. *Devil-drawer.* An incompetent artist. L17–M19. *Devil's smiles.* Unsettled April weather. 19–20. *Devil's tattoo.* 'Beating with one's foot against the ground, as done by persons in low spirits' (Egan). 19. See also *Gaudy.*

Devotional habits. 'Horses weak in the knees, and apt to stumble and fall, are said to have these' (Hotten). M–L19.

Dewdrops. Coal thrown at a hobo on a train (us). E20.

Dibble. A moustache. 17.

Dick. A dictionary. 19. *Doddering dick.* A machine gun (wwii). M20. See also *Swallow the dick.*

Dicky. A woman's slip or under-petticoat. L18–19. *Dicky Sam.* A Liverpudlian, or Scouser. M–L19.

Diddle. Gin. M18–E19.

Dido. An overdressed woman. M20.

Die. Die dunghill. Display contrition when faced with the gallows. M18–M19. *Die of acceleration.* Starve to death in an uncharitable world. L19–E20. *Die the death of a trooper's horse.* Be hanged (and so die with one's shoes on). L18–E19.

Digger's delight. A broad-brimmed felt hat favoured by New Zealand gold prospectors. L19–20.

Dildock. A gambler who relies on marked cards (US). E20.

Dimber-damber. 'A top man, or prince, among the canting crew; also the chief rogue of the gang' (B.E.). L17–19.

Dimmock. Money. E–M19.

Ding. Drop the acquaintance of a person suddenly. L–M19. *Ding-bat.* 1. The physical expression of a mother's love for her children. L19. 2. A common tramp (US). E20. *Ding-boy.* 'A rogue, a hector, a bully, or sharper' (B.E.). L17–18. *Ding-donger.* A hyperactive American. E20.

Dingo. Mildly mentally disturbed (WWI). E20.

Dinkum. 1. Hard work (AUS). L19–20. 2. An Australian veteran of the Gallipoli campaign (WWI). E20.

Dinnyhayser. An Australian sockdolager (q.v.). L19–20.

Dipsey. A stint in the workhouse (US). E20.

Dirty. Dirty-shirt march. A relaxed Sunday-morning stroll before dressing smartly for lunch. L19–E20. *Dirty thing.* An adolescent girls' term for an amorous teenage boy. M19–20.

Discumgalligumfricated. Pleasantly surprised (US). E20.

Dishclout, make a napkin of one's. Marry one's cook. M18–19.

Dishybilly. A state of casual dress or dishabille (US). E20.

Dismal ditty. 'The psalm sung by the felons at the gallows, just before they are turned off' (*Lex.Bal.*). L17–E19.

Dittos. A suit all of the same colour and cloth. 19–E20.

Do a Chloë. Appear naked in public (AUS). L19–20.

Docked smack smooth. 'One who has suffered an amputation of his penis, from a venereal complaint' (Grose). M18–19.

Dock-whalloping. The pastime of sauntering round a waterfront admiring the ships moored at dockside. L19–20.

Doctor Johnson. The penis (perhaps because of the size of the Great Cham's *dick* (q.v.)?). L18–L19.

Doddies. An utterly self-centred individual. L19–E20.

Dodo. Disrespectful name for the Metropolitan Police. L19.

Dog. As much needs it as a dog does a side pocket. A phrase used when someone desires something inessential. L18–E20. *Dog and maggot*. A biscuit with cheese. E–M20. *Doggery*. 1. Blatant cheating. 2. Absurd behaviour. M19–E20. *Doggy*. 1. A cavalry officer's servant. M19. 2. Elegant. L19–M20. *Dog in a doublet*. A stalwart, courageous individual. 16–E19. *Dog robbers*. The tweed suitings favoured by officers on leave (WWII). M20. *Dogs*. Sausages. M19–20. *Dog's body*. A sailor's pease pudding. 19. *Dog's nose*. Gin and beer. E–M19. *Dog's rig*. Have sex until reduced to exhaustion, then ignore one's partner. M18–19. *Dog's vomit*. A seafarers' treat: ship's biscuit and meat hashed together. L19–20. *Dog-walloping*. The practice of picking up the discarded ends of cigars and cigarettes for personal consumption. E–M19. *Fog dog*. The bottom part of a rainbow. M19–20. *Like a butcher's dog*, 'i.e. lie by the beef without touching it: a simile often applicable to married men' (*Lex.Bal.*). L18–E19. *Tie up a dog with sausages*. Be staggeringly indiscreet (US). E20. See also *90 dog*; *Noisy-dog racket*; *Sunday dog*.

Dolly. Dolly-mop. 'A semi-professional street-walker' (Hotten). M19. *Dolly-worship*. Roman Catholicism (i.e. idolatry). L19–E20.

Do me goods. Woodbine cigarettes. E–M20.

Dommerer. 'A beggar pretending that his tongue has been cut out by the Algerines, or cruel and bloody-thirsty Turks, or else that he was born deaf and dumb' (Grose). 16–18.

Donegan worker. A thief who targets men in public conveniences and washrooms (US). 19–E20.

Donkey ball. A game of baseball in which the players all have to ride donkeys (US). E20.

Donk's ding-bat. An Australian army mule-attendant. E–M20.

Doofunnies. The contents of a cowboy's pockets (US). E20.

Dook. An enormous nose (in honour of the first Duke of Wellington's distinguished proboscis). E19–E20.

Dookin-cove. A fortune-teller. M19.

Door-mat. A luxurious beard, particularly one at the vanguard of the mid-Victorian 'beard movement'. M–L19.

Dopey. The mistress of a thief (US). 19–E20.

Dorbie. An initiate into a secret society. M–L19.

Dork. A thick slice of bread. L19–E20.

Dossy. Stylish, elegant. L19.

Double. Double-breasted water-butt smasher. A man with an awe-inspiring physique. L19–E20. *Double-hocked.* Fat-ankled. M–L19. *Double jugg.* A man's backside. L17–19. *Double-shung.* (Of a man) well endowed. 19–20.

Doughy-nose. A lovestruck sea-dog. L19–E20.

Drag the pudding. Be dismissed from one's job just prior to Christmas. L19.

Drain. 'Gin: so called from the diuretic qualities imputed to that liquor' (*Lex.Bal.*). 19.

Draw the King's picture. Coin counterfeit money. L18–M19.

Dreadnought. A sailors' condom (WWII). M20. *Dreadnoughts.* Women's flannel undergarments, substantial and snug-fitting. E–M20.

Dredgy. The ghost of a drowned sailor. L19–E20.

Drinking-time. 'Four o'clock, usually' (Bee). E–M19.

Driver's pint. A gallon. L19–20.

Drops. Gin; spirits more generally. E–M19.

Drummer. A thief who drugs his victims. M19.

Drummond. An infallible scheme (from the 'respectable banking-house', Drummond & Co.). E–M19.

Drunk as an emperor, 'i.e. ten times as drunk as a lord' (Egan). E–M19.

Duchess. 'A woman enjoyed with her pattens on, or by a man in boots' (Grose). L18–L19.

Duck. Do a duck. Hide under a seat while on public transport to avoid buying a ticket. L19. *Duck disease.* The affliction of tiny little legs (WWI). E20. *Duck-fucker.* The sailor responsible for the poultry on board a warship. M18–E19. *Duck-shover.* A pushy Australian cab-driver. M–L19. *Fake the duck.* Adulterate or water down alcoholic drinks. M–L19. *Like a dying duck in a thunderstorm.* Apathetic and crestfallen. M–L19. See also *German duck, Lame duck.*

Duddering rake. 'A thundering rake … one devilishly lewd' (B.E.). L17–E19.

Dude. A fastidiously foppish man – a bit of a metrosexual (US). L19–E20. *Dude train.* A train service charging a supplementary fare (US). E20. *Dudes.* Clothes. M16–20.

Duffer. 1. A trader who passes off damaged or old goods as smuggled ones at inflated prices. M18–M19. 2. A female smuggler. 19. 3. A worthless gold mine (AUS, NZ). M–L19.

Duffy. 1. A quarter-pint of gin. E–M19. 2. A West Indian ghost. 19. *Duke.* Gin. M–L19.

Dullmajor. An interpreter in a POW camp (WWI). E20.

Dumb watch. 'A bubo in the groin' (Grose). M18–E19.

Dummee-hunter. A thief of gentlemen's wallets. E19–E20.

Dundreary. A brainless bewhiskered beau. M–L19.

Dungaree-settler. A penniless emigrant in Australia. M19.

Durrynacker. A wandering female lace-seller and fortune-teller. M19–E20.

Dutch. Dutch comfort. It could be worse. L18–19. *Dutch feast.* An entertainment where the host gets drunk before his guests. L18–L19. *Dutchman's anchor.* Anything vital which, when suddenly needed, is discovered to have been left at home. M19–E20. *Dutchman's breeks.* Small faint patches of blue in an otherwise overcast sky. M–L19.

Eagle-hawk. Remove the wool from dead sheep (AUS). L19.

Early doors. Women's knickers. L19–20.

Eat toot. Become accustomed to life in New Zealand. 19–20.

EC women. City bankers' wives. L19.

Eel-skins. Figure-hugging trousers or skirts. 19.

Elephant. A life-changing experience. M19–20. *Bang through the elephant.* Thoroughly versed in the arts of debauchery. L19–E20. *Bang up to the elephant.* Faultless. L19–E20. *See the elephant.* Be seduced. L19.

Empress-pidgin. A conversation with Queen Victoria. M–L19.

English. English disease. 1. Depression. 18–19. 2. Rickets. M–L19. *English pluck.* Money. L19–E20.

Evening wheezes. The patent nonsense peddled by evening newspapers to boost circulation. L19–E20.

Exasperate. 'Over-aspirate the letter H, or aspirate it whenever it commences a word, as is commonly done by under-educated people who wish to show off their breeding' (Hotten). M–L19.

Execution day. Washing day. L17–E20.

Explosion. The birth of a child. M–L19.

Export trade. The white-slave trade to Argentina. L19.

Eye. Eye-opener. A homosexual (US). 20. *Eye-water.* Gin. 19.

Face-making. Procreation. M18–E19.

Faddee. Fish that are no longer fresh. E–M19.

Fadoodling. Sexual intercourse. 17.

Faggot. 1. 'A term of opprobrium used by low people to children and women' (Hotten). E17–L19. 2. 'A man hired at a muster to appear as a soldier' (Grose). 18–19.

Fair trader. A smuggler. E–M18.

Fairy. An unpleasantly licentious old woman. L19–E20.

Fake boodle. An ostentatiously waved wad of cash, in which the high-denomination note on the outside conceals blank paper (US). L19. See also *Boodle.*

Fall for a seven-up. Be convicted of burglarising a convenience store (US). E20.

Famillionaire. The manner in which very wealthy men bestow their patronage. L19.

Family. Family disturbance. Whisky. 19. *Family man.* A receiver of stolen goods. L18–E20.

Fancy. Fancy man. One kept by a prostitute, 'a petticoat pensioner'. L18–E19. *Fancy sash.* A punch (AUS). L19.

Farcy gambs. Legs swollen or covered in sores. L18–E19.

Farthing-taster. A tiny ice cream. L19–E20.

Farting crackers. A pair of breeches. L17–18.

Fash one's beard. Become annoyed. L18.

Fat as a hen in the forehead. A phrase used to describe a particularly thin person. E17–E19.

Feague. A horse-trader's trick in which a piece of ginger (or a live eel) is stuck up a horse's backside to make it act in a lively manner. Hence, to encourage someone. L18–E19.

Feel the collar. Break into a sweat while walking. L19–E20.

Feisty breeches. A deadly insult to a small boy. 19.

Femme ork. A group of female musicians (US). E20.

Ferricadouzer. A knock-out punch. M19.

Fetch mettle. 'The act of self pollution' (Grose). L18–19.

Fibbing. In boxing, the hitting of an opponent when held defenceless 'in Chancery', i.e. a headlock. E–M19.

Fice or *Foyse.* 'A small windy escape backwards, more obvious to the nose than ears; frequently by old ladies charged on their lap-dogs' (*Lex.Bal.*). L18–19.

Fiddle. Fiddle-face. Someone with an unusually wizened countenance. M–L19. *Fiddler's green.* 'The place where sailors expect to go when they die. It is a place of fiddling, dancing, rum, and tobacco' (Hotten). L18–19.

Field-running. The erection of poor-quality new-build developments on green-field sites. M19–E20.

Fight. Fighting nob work. 'To act with such prudence and knowledge of the world, as to prosper and become independent without any labour or bodily exertion' (Egan). E–M19. *Fight space with a hairpin.* Attempt the impossible. L19–E20. *Fight the tiger.* Play with American gamblers – 'a dangerous pastime' (Hotten). M–L19.

Fig-leaf. A small apron worn by women. M–L19.

Figure-dancer. An individual who alters the face value of cheques, banknotes, etc. L19–E20.

Fillibrush. Praise insincerely or ironically. M–L19.

Finger. Finger-mob. A criminal gang operating under police protection (US). E20. *Finger-post.* A parson: 'like the finger-post, he points out a way he has never been and probably will never go, i.e. the way to heaven' (Grose). L18–19. *Finger-smith.* 1. A pickpocket. 19. 2. A midwife. E19–E20.

Fire a gun. Clumsily shoehorn a subject into conversation. L18–19.

Firkytoodle. Indulge in foreplay. 17–19.

Fisgig. The comedy to be derived from the appearance of someone's face. E19.

Fish. Fish-bagger. A well-to-do individual who does all their food shopping in town on the way home from work, rather than giving their trade to local small businesses. L19. *Fish-fosh.* Kedgeree. L19.

Fit. Fit as a pudding. Completely fit for purpose. L16–17. *Not fit the head.* A phrase describing a good piece of work initially rejected by a client which, when resubmitted unchanged, is accepted with delight. 19.

Fizzed in the fist. Branded on the hand. 17.

Flamp. Sell off army property illegally. L19–20.

Flanderkin. A hugely fat man or horse. L17–18.

Flannel. Hot gin and beer, spiced with nutmeg and sweetened with sugar. L18–M19. (Also *Hot flannel.*)

Flapdoodler. A windbag politician. L19–E20.

Flapper. 1. A slow and clumsy rider to hounds. M–L19. 2. 'A very immoral young girl in her early "teens" ' (Ware). L19–E20. 3. A piece of canvas with a wooden handle for dispersing poison gas (WWI). E20. *Flapperese.* The unintelligible argot of teenage American girls (US). E20. *Flappers.* The immensely pointed fashionable shoes favoured by popular musicians. L19. *Flapper's bracket.* A motorcycle pillion. M20. See also *Grand-flapper.*

Flash. Flash-lingo. Underworld slang. L18–19. *Flashman.* 1. One who speaks flash-lingo. L18–19. 2. A man who lives off a prostitute's earnings. L18–E20. 3. A bouncer for a brothel. 19. 4. A patron of pugilism. M19. *Flash of lightning.* A glass of gin. L18–M19. (Also *Streak of lightning.* M19–20.) *Flash-tail.* A toffer (q.v.). M19. *Flash the drag.* Adopt feminine attire for illicit purposes. M–L19.

Flay. Flay-bottomist. A bum-brusher (q.v.). L18–19. *Flay the fox.* Be as sick as a parrot. L16–19.

Flimp. 1. Hustle, or rob. E19. 2. Have sexual intercourse. M19. *Put on the flimp.* Garotte someone for their money. E–M19.

Flink. Fail to live up to one's responsibilities because of a lack of moral courage (US). 19.

Flip. A hot mixture of small beer, brandy and sugar. L17–19.

Flirt. A female student (US). E20.

Flitterati. 'Superficial pretenders to literary interest and taste' (Weseen) (US). E20.

Floater. A faux pas. E20. *Floaters.* Dumplings and stew (WWI). E20.

Flop. A complete and utter volte-face in political policy (US). L19–E20. *Flop-whop.* A heavy fall. L19.

Florence. A young woman careless of her appearance. L17–18.

Flossy. A woman older than her male partner (AUS). L19–20.

Flounce. An unsubtle application of eye-liner. M19–E20.

Flounder. A drowned person's body. L19.

Flourish, take a. Take a flyer (q.v.). M18–19.

Flowery. A prison cell. L19–E20.

Flue-faker. 1. A chimney-sweep. 19. 2. A petty gambler (i.e. one who bets on the great sweep[stake]s). M19–E20.

Fluence, put on the. Bend to one's will. M–L19.

Fluff. Short-change someone. L19. *Fluffy.* Drunk and incapable. L19.

Fly. Fly a kite. 1. Pick up a whore. L17–E18. 2. Take one's leave (especially from lodgings) via the window. M19. *Fly-flapped.* Be flogged in the pillory or at the cart's tail. L18–M19. *Flying camp.* Beggars who gang together en masse to target funerals. L17–E19. *Flying pig.* A large mortar bomb (WWI). E20. *Flying trapeze.* First World War cheese. E20. *Fly-jerks.* The corks suspended from a hat-brim to ward off flies (AUS). L19–20. *Take a flyer.* 'Enjoy a woman with her clothes on, or without going to bed' (Grose). L18–M19.

Follow a whereas. Be declared bankrupt (after the newspaper notice to that effect which begins, 'Whereas …'). E–M19.

Foo foo. An American sailors' term for perfume. L19–E20.

Foont. A sovereign, twenty shillings. M19.

Foot wabbler. 'A contemptuous appellation for a foot soldier, commonly used by the cavalry' (Grose). L18–M19.

Footy. Utterly worthless, beyond contempt. M18–L19.

Foozle. A tedious old bore. M19.

Fop-doodle. An idiot, or waste of space. M–L17.

Fopper. A mistake. L19.

Forced-meat. 'Something inherently unpleasant endured under compulsion' (Partridge) – defined by Bee as having to forego a glass of gin for lack of money. E–M19.

Ford children. Illegitimate offspring (US). M20.

Fornicators. Old-fashioned trousers with a large flap fastening at the front instead of a fly. M–L19.

Fortune-teller. A judge. L17–E19.

Forty. Forty guts. An overweight man; a superchub. M19. *Forty-pounder.* A policeman (from the bounty awarded for apprehending a murderer). E19.

Fourth of July. A shoot-out between criminals (US). E–M20.

Fox's paw, make a. 1. Commit a social gaffe. L18–19. 2. (Of a woman) carelessly allow oneself to be seduced. L18–19.

Franc-fileur. A reluctant male participant at a ball. L19–E20.

Frater. A beggar who uses 'sham patents' or false petitions in aid of a good cause to earn money. M16–E20.

Fray Bentos. Very well, usually in response to the question 'How are you?' (cf. *très bien*) (WWI). E20.

Free. Free-holder. 'He whose wife goes with him to the ale-house' (B.E.). M17–E19. *Free of fumbler's hall.* Said of a man unable to make his wife pregnant. L18–E19.

French. 'Term used in Maryland and Virginia for any fashion that is disliked' (Ware). 19. *Drive French horses.* Vomit (from the characteristic cry of Gallic wagon-drivers, '*Hue donc!*'). M19–E20. *French gout.* The pox. 17–19.

Friday-face. A gloomy-featured person. L16–L19.

Frig-pig. 'A trifling, fiddle-faddle fellow' (*Lex.Bal.*). L18–E19.

Frilled lizard. A bewhiskered Australian. 20.

Frisk a lob. Rob a shop's till. M18–E19.

Frog. A policeman. M–L19. *Frog action.* Bicycle polo. L19–E20. *Froglander.* A Dutchman. 17. *Frog-skin.* A condom (AUS). E–M20. *Frog's wine.* Gin. E–M19.

Frosy. A treat 'eaten quietly by not more than two, after the children are in bed'. L19–E20.

Fruit. An obliging woman, i.e. easy pickings (US). E20.

Frummagemmed. Strangled, or hanged. M17–M19.

Frumper. A stout fellow. E–M19.

Fubsey. Delightfully plump - a term of endearment. M17–20.

Fuddyduddy. An effeminate man (US). E20.

Fug pants. Thick underwear worn by schoolboys. M20.

Fulham virgin. A woman of easy virtue. 19.

Fuller's earth. Gin (and bitters). E–M19.

Fun and frolics. Testicles (rhyming slang). E–M20.

Funker. A prostitute who shirks in unpleasant weather. M–L19.

Furphy. An unfounded rumour (AUS). E–M20.

Furry-tail. A non-union worker; one likely to undercut trade-union wages. M–L19.

Fussocks. 'A lazy fat-arsed wench' (B.E.). L17–19.

Fustilugs. 1. A woman with hygiene issues. L17–19. 2. A very untidy child. 18–19.

Futilitarian. An unmitigated pessimist or doom-merchant (US). E20.

Futter. A New Zealand storeroom on stilts. 19–20.

Fuzz. Shuffle playing cards very thoroughly. M18–E19. *Fuzzy-tail.* A tramp in a foul mood (US). E20.

Gadarening. Extravagantly self-destructive behaviour (US). 19–20.

Gad the hoof. Walk about barefoot. M19.

Gagarino. A highly lurid, improvised drama. M–L19.

Gaggers. 1. 'Cheats, who by sham pretences, and wonderful stories of their sufferings, impose on the credulity of well meaning people' (*Lex.Bal.*). L18–M19. 2. In the USA, men who pimp their wives. 19–20.

Galbe. An unfortunate person whose features, when seen in profile, appear violently unpleasant. L19.

Galley-slang. 'A landsman's attempt at nautical jargon' (Bowen). L19–E20.

Galligaskins. A pair of breeches. 18–19.

Gallivant. 1. 'A nest of whores' (Bee). E19. 2. 'To wait upon the ladies' (Hotten). M–L19.

Gally. 'Frighten or alarm by hideous means' (Bee). E–M19.

Galoot. A recruit, or clumsy soldier; a likely member of the awkward squad (q.v.). E–M19.

Gammocks. Vigorous revelling; painting the town red. 19.

Gamp. A large umbrella that fails to fold away neatly. M–L19.

Gander month. 'That month in which a man's wife lies in: wherefore, during that time, husbands plead a sort of indulgence in matters of gallantry' (*Lex.Bal.*). M17–E19.

Garden. Gardener. A clumsy, nervous coachman; a bad driver. M–L19. *Put in the garden.* Defraud someone of their fair share of a mutual endeavour. E–M19.

Garnish. 'An entrance fee demanded by the old prisoners of one just committed to gaol' (Grose). L16–M19.

Garret election. 'A ludicrous ceremony practised every new parliament: it consists of a mock election of two members to represent the borough of Garret (a few straggling cottages, near Wandsworth, in Surrey). The qualification of a voter is having enjoyed a woman in the open air within that district' (Grose). 18–E19.

Garrison hack. A soldiers' whore. M–L19.

Gas. Gaseous. 'Liable to "flare up" at any offence' (Hotten). M–L19. *Gas-pipe.* 1. A steamship with very fast lines. L19–E20. 2. A rifle. L19–E20.

Gaudy. Neat but not gaudy, as the devil said when he painted his bottom pink and tied up his tail with pea-green ribbon. A disapproving comment directed at older women who like to wear unflatteringly bright colours. 19.

Gay. Gaying instrument. A man's penis. 19. *Gay tyke boy.* A dog-fancier. M19. *Gay woman.* A prostitute or mistress. 19.

Geebung. 'An unsophisticated, uncultured, philistine native-born Australian, who values material gain above everything else' (Green). M19–20.

Geek. A snake charmer; a carnival freak who bites the heads off live chickens (US). E20.

Geezer. A fix of drugs or strong drink (US). E–M20.

Geneva. Gin. 17–18. (Also *Geneva print.*)

Gentleman. A crowbar. M–L19. *Gentleman in black.* The devil. M17–19. *Gentleman of (the) three ins.* 'In debt, in gaol, and in danger of remaining there for life: or, in gaol, indicted, and in danger of being hanged in chains' (*Lex.Bal.*). L18–M19.

Gentleman's master. A highwayman (because they obey his command to stand and deliver). L18–M19.

German. German duck. 1. 'Half a sheep's head boiled with onions' (Grose). L18–L19. 2. A bed-bug. M–L19. *German gospel.* Vain, boasting megalomania. L19.

Germany, made in. Of inferior quality. L19–E20.

Ghoul. A blackmailer who preys upon women (US). M19–E20.

Gibberish. Thieves' and gypsies' slang. 16–E19.

Giggle. Giggle mug. A never-endingly cheerful countenance (profoundly irritating). L19–E20. *Giggle pants.* Trousers for working in (AUS). M20. *Giggle stick.* A man's penis (US). M20.

Gig-lamps. Spectacles; one who wears them. M–L19.

Gill. A man 'who pokes in his nose unasked, as if authoritatively' (Bee). E–M19. *Gill-flurt.* 'A proud minx, a vain capricious woman' (Grose). 17–19.

Gimper. A hotshot aeroplane pilot (US). E20.

Ginicomtwig. Have sexual intercourse. L16–E17.

Gink. An unpopular person (US). E20.

Gin-spinner. 1. A distiller. L18–L19. 2. A wine vault. M–L19.

Giraffe. 1. Bamboozle (US). M19. 2. Someone who indulges 'in necking' (US). E20.

Give. Give a floater to. Give someone forty-eight hours to get out of town (US). E–M20. *Give a girl a green gown.* 'Tumble her on the grass, and pick the pins out of her frock' (Egan). L16–E19. *Give jaro.* Reprimand or insult (NZ). 20. *Give Kennedy* (or *Neddy*). Smack someone hard, if not fatally, with a poker. M19. *Give nature a fillip.* Indulge in wine and women (song seemingly optional). L17–19. *Give turnips.* Break off an acquaintance heartlessly; jilt. E19.

Gladstone. Cheap claret (the GOM reduced duties on French wines). M–L19. *Gladstonise.* Prevaricate at great length while giving nothing away. L19.

Glass arm. A repetitive strain injury suffered by telegraph operators (US). E20.

Glazier. A thief who breaks shop windows or display cabinets in order to steal their contents. L18–E19.

Glims, puff the. Make an old horse appear younger by injecting air into the collapsed tissues in the hollows over its eyes in order to fill them out. M–L19.

Gluepot. 'A parson, from joining men and women together in matrimony' (Grose). L18–19.

Gnarler. A small, noisy watch-dog. E19–E20.

Go. A bowl of gin and water. L18–E19. *Go barpoo.* Lose one's nerve, go mad; crash one's aeroplane (WWI). E20. *Go-by-the-ground.* A vertically challenged individual. 18–19. *Go for the gloves.* Bet recklessly on horses. L19. *Go on the batter.* Binge-drink (WWI). E20. *Go sideways.* Engage in criminal activities. L19. *Go to Putney.* Go to hell! M19. *Go to Sausage Hill.* Be taken prisoner (WWI). E20. *Go trumpet-cleaning.* Die. L19–E20.

Goat. 1. The fundament. M19. 2. Thrash. M19–E20. *Look like a billy goat in stays.* Appear ridiculous (if not unnatural). L19. *Ride the goat.* Be initiated into the Masons or other secret society. L19. *Run like a hairy goat,* i.e. with a lot of effort but little speed (AUS). M20.

Gob. Gobbie. A coastguard. L19. *Gob-shite.* 1. A lump of used chewing tobacco (US). L19–E20. 2. An American sailor. E20. *Gob-spud.* A potato stuffed in one's mouth in order to fill out one's hollow cheeks as an aid to shaving. L19.

God. An Etonian sixth-former. M–L19. *God-father.* One who picks up the tab for the rest of the company. L18–19. *God-forbid.* A child. L19–20. *God's mercy.* Bacon and eggs. 19.

Goggled goblin. A night-fighter pilot (WWII). M20.

Gold. Gold-brick. 1. Sham sickness in order to get out of work, malinger (US). M19–20. 2. Rip someone off (US). M19–20. *Gold finder.* A night-soil or 'tom-turd' man. 17–E19. *Gold-headed dick.* An ornate riding crop. M19.

Golgotha. A hat (from 'the place of the skull'). M19.

Goliath. A person with absolutely no taste or interest in the arts – a complete philistine. L19–E20.

Gollion. A lump of phlegm (AUS). 20.

Gommy. A would-be wit: the sort 'who calls Mr Gladstone a GOM, and thinks he has made a good joke'. L19.

Gonger. 1. An opium pipe or addict (US). E–M20. 2. A policeman patrolling by car (US). M20.

Goober. Goober-grabber. An American rustic. 19–20. *Hang a goober.* Kiss a woman (US). E20.

Good woman. A quiet one. E19.

Goozlum. Something passing for gravy (US). 20.

Gopher mob. A gang of thieves who specialise in tunnelling into bank vaults (US). L19–M20.

Gorger. A gentleman, or smartly dressed man. 19. *Rotten gorger.* A boy who loiters round Covent Garden in order to satisfy his craving for discarded fruit. L19.

Gormagon. A man and a woman sharing a horse (from their resemblance to a bewildering hermaphroditic monster). 18.

Gospel. Gospel-gab. Insincere proselytising. L19. *Gospel-grinder.* A Sunday-school teacher. M19.

Gossoon. A boy (cf. French *garçon*). M–L19.

Goth. A complete idiot. M19.

Gouge. 'Squeeze out a man's eye with the thumb: a cruel practice used by the Bostonians in America' (Grose). L18–E19.

Government. Government man. A convict (AUS). M19. *Government securities.* Handcuffs. M–L19.

Grabben gullen pie. 'A dish made of a scooped out pumpkin stuffed with possum meat and then baked' (Baker, Aus.). 19–20.

Grabeteria. A supermarket or self-service café (US). E20.

Grand-flapper. An older woman who copies teenage fashions and behaviour; mutton dressed as lamb (US). E–M20.

Granny. Disguise oneself (NB the wolf in 'Little Red Riding Hood'). E20. See also *See one's grandmother.*

Grave-digger, like a, i.e. 'up to the arse in business, and don't know which way to turn' (*Lex.Bal.*). L18–M19.

Gravel-rash, have the. Extremely drunk, legless. M–L19.

Gravesend twins. Pieces of solid sewage. M–L19.

Gravy. Gravy-eyed. Blear-eyed or rheumy. L18–19. *Gravy-hound.* A patient in an American prison sickbay. E20.

Grease a fat sow in the arse. Attempt to bribe a wealthy man. 18–M19.

Grecian bend. The teetering gait and inelegant posture caused by wearing very high-heeled boots. M–L19.

Greek. An Irishman. M19.

Greenhouse. A London bus (from the amount of glass in the windows). L19–E20.

Gregorian tree. The gallows (probably after a hangman in James I's time, Gregory Brandon, and his son and successor, 'young Gregory'). M17–E19.

Grey. A coin with two heads or two tails, used to trick the gullible. 19. *Grey-beard.* Dutch earthenware jugs used for smuggling gin. L18–E19. *Greys.* Ennui; uncontrollable yawning. M19–E20.

Griddle. 'Sing hymns in the street as a means of attracting sympathy' (Irwin) (US). M–L19.

Gridiron. A county-court summons. M19.

Griffin. 1. A greenhorn, or newby. 19–E20. 2. An umbrella. 3. A tip-off, usually of trouble (WWI). E20.

Grim. Grimness. Literature which tries to be erotic. L19. *On the grim.* Military service on the Indian north-west frontier with Afghanistan. E–M20.

Grimp. A numbskull (US). 19–20.

Grin in a glass case. Be anatomised for murder (the remains of executed criminals were often dissected). M18–M19.

Grog-blossoms. Blemishes to the complexion brought on by hard drinking. L18–L19.

Gromet. A ship's boy. 17.

Groovy. Set in one's ways. L19.

Groping for Jesus. Embarrassingly fervent public prayer. L19.

Ground-hog day. Armistice Day, 11 November 1918, i.e. the day when everyone left their holes (US). E–M20.

Grub Street news. Deliberately made-up news. L17–E19.

Grunter's gig. A smoked pig's face. L18–M19.

Guanoing the mind. The result of reading trashy novels or chick-lit. M19.

Guardsman's wriggle. An 'exaggerated salute affected by the Guards' (*Soldiers' Slang*). E20.

Gubber. A beachcomber at work. M19–20.

Gublungssit. The name of a station as it sounds when read out over a railway PA-system (US). E–M20.

Guffoon. A clumsy oaf. M–L19.

Gugusse. 'An effeminate youth who frequents the private company of priests' (Ware). L19.

Guinea-pig. A non-executive company director who does little other than attend board meetings; a fat-cat. L19.

Gull-groper. Unscrupulous money-lenders who hit on desperate gamblers. 17–E19.

Gully-fluff. 'The waste – coagulated dust, crumbs, and hair – which accumulates imperceptibly in the pockets of schoolboys' (Hotten). M–L19. Cf. *Beggars' velvet.*

Gum. Gum-puncher. An Australian dentist. 20. *Gum-sucker.* An Australian idiot. M–L19. *Gummy.* Fat, particularly with reference to the ankles of men, women and horses. M18–L19.

Gump. A scrawny or diseased chicken (US). E–M20.

Gundiguts. 'A fat pursy fellow' (B.E.); a lard-arse. L17–M19.

Gussey. A person suffering from overindulgence (US). E20.

Gut-foundered. Hungry to the point of faintness. M17–M19.

Gutter-lane. The throat. 17–19.

Guttle. Consume alcoholic beverages. E18.

Guy. A dark lantern (after Guy Fawkes). E–M19.

Guzinters. An animal's innards (AUS). E–M20.

Hackslaver. Stammer or stutter. M–L19.

Haddock. A purse. E–M19.

Haggis debate. A parliamentary discussion devoted to Scottish affairs. L19–E20.

Hakim. A doctor. M19.

Half. Half-an-Oxford. Half a crown (*2s. 6d.*). L19. (Also a *Half-tusherroon.* M19.) *Half a surprise.* A single black eye. L19–E20. *Half-rocked.* Very stupid. M19.

Hallelujah gallop. A rousing hymn. L19–E20.

Hallion. A disreputable unemployed valet. L18–L19.

Hamburg. A false rumour. L19–20.

Hammered. Married. L19–E20.

Hampsteads. Teeth. L19–M20.

Hand-basket portion. A woman whose husband is financially supported by her family. L18–M19.

Hang. Hang in the bell-ropes. Put off one's marriage after the banns have been read (i.e. very late in the day). M18–L19. *Hang one's latch-pan.* Pout sulkily. 19–20.

Hank. 'Cessation from any work or duty, on the score of indisposition, or some other pretence' (Egan). 19.

Hans Wurst. A German Tommy Atkins (wwi). E20.

Happy. Happy as a boxing kangaroo in fog-time. In the Slough of Despond (aus). 20. *Happy as ducks in Arizona.* Miserable (us). E–M20. *Happy family.* 'A quiet cageful of mutually destructive animals' (*Slang*). M19–E20.

Hard. Hard-baked. Constipated. 19. *Hard-puncher.* A fur cap in fashion with London thugs. L19–E20. *Hard Simpson.* Ice. M19. *Hard-up.* A dog-end seller. M19.

Harriet Lane. 'Australian canned meat – because it had the appearance of chopped-up meat; and Harriet Lane was chopped up by one Wainwright' (Ware). L19.

Harry crashers. Sleep (wwii). M20.

Hasty-pudding. An illegitimate child. M–L19.

Hatter. A solitary Australian miner. M–L19.

Head-robber. 1. A plagiarist. L19–E20. 2. A butler. L19–M20.

Heart's ease. Gin. L17–M19.

Heathen philosopher. One whose backside can be seen through the holes in his breeches. L17–18.

Heaver. A robber specialising in the theft of tradesmen's account books. L18–E19.

Heavy baggage. A woman with children. L18–19.

Hedge-creeper. A laundry thief. M16–E19.

Hedgehog. 1. A boat propelled by numerous oars. 19. 2. Veal. M–L19. 3. A devious or greedy individual (us). E–M20.

Heigh-ho. Pilfered yarn. M19–E20.

Hell. 1. The hiding place in which a tailor conceals the cloth, etc., he has stolen from his employer. L18–E19. 2. A West End gambling den. L18–M19.

Hen frigate. A house where the woman rules the roost. 18–19.

Hep. Well informed, sophisticated (us). 20.

Hickey. Mildly inebriated, to the point of hiccoughs. L18–19.

High. 1. Drunk. E17–E20. 2. Venereally diseased. L19. *High-flyer.* A slave-ship. L19–20. *High jinks.* 'A gambler at dice, who, having a strong head, drinks to intoxicate his adversary, or pigeon' (Grose). M18–E19. *High living.* 'To lodge in a garret, or cockloft' (*Lex.Bal.*). L18–19. *High-lows.* 'Shoes which reach to the ankles: they have a thievish aspect' (Bee). 19. *High monkey-monk.* A very (self-)important person (US). 19. *High-toby.* A highwayman. 18–E19.

Hill-top literature. Sound advice, from 'danger-board warnings to cyclists on the summits of steep hills' (Ware). L19–E20.

Hip-hop. Hoppingly. L17.

Hippo. An emetic (particularly ipecacuanha). E20. *Hippoed.* Fooled, deceived (US). L19–20.

Hit. Hit the hot bozel. Binge-drink (US). E–M20. *Hit the hump.* Attempt to break out of an American prison. E–M20.

Hittites. The crowd and participants at a boxing match. E19–E20.

Hobberdehoy. A youth halfway between man and boy, an awkward adolescent. M16–L19.

Hobbledygee. 'A pace between a walk and a run' (*Lex.Bal.*). L18–L19.

Hockey. The state of inebriation brought on by drinking stale beer. L18–L19.

Hocus. 'Stupify a person by putting opium or some other drug in his liquor, and when he is asleep robbing him' (Brandon). 19.

Hoddy-doddy. 1. A small dumpy individual, or short-arse. M16–L19. 2. The revolving light in a lighthouse. L19–20.

Hog. Hog-grubber. 1. 'A close-fisted, narrow-soul'd sneaking Fellow' (B.E.). L17–E19. 2. A licensed Thames waterman. M–L19. *Hog in armour.* 1. A lumpish man or woman wearing inappropriately fashionable or fine clothes. M17–19. 2. A sailors' term for an ironclad warship. M–L19.

Hoga, that won't! That won't do! 'One of the commonest of the Anglo-Indian slang phrases' (Hotten). M–L19.

Hogo. Pungently flavoured or scented. M17–19.

Hoist-lay. Stealing a man's money by shaking him upside down until his pockets empty. M–L19.

Hoity-toity. 'A giddy, thoughtless, romping girl' (*Lex.Bal.*). L17–E19.

Hole. Can't see a hole through a ladder. Blind drunk. M–L19. *Hole in the head.* One's mouth (US). 19–E20. *Hole in the wall.* An unlicensed bar or liquor store (US). 19.

Holiday. A patch left unpainted by a decorator. 19–20.

Holland. Hollanders. Pointy waxed moustaches. L19. *Holland tape.* Gin. M18.

Holy lamb. In Ireland, a complete villain. M18–L19.

Home. Home rulers. Baked potatoes. L19. *Homey.* An Englishman, especially one newly emigrated (AUS, NZ). E–M20.

Homitosis. Excruciatingly bad taste when it comes to home improvement (US). E–M20.

Homo. A man. M19.

Hondey. A Mancunian omnibus. M–L19.

Hoof and mouth disease. Golf (US). E–M20.

Hoo-ha. An artillery bombardment (WWI). E20.

Hooker. 1. A term of affection used by a seaman for his ship. M–L19. 2. A stealer of pocket-watches. L19.

Hoosh. A thick nourishing soup, the staple diet of polar explorers. E20.

Hoot. Hoot-balloo. A voluble Irish shout of alarm. 'He who has not heard the Irish *hoot*, has a pleasure to come' (Bee). 19. *Hooting pudding.* A plum pudding containing so few plums that they have to hoot to one another in order to locate their fellows across the echoing void. M19–E20.

Hop. Hop-merchant. A dancing master. L17–19. *Hopper-arsed.* Fat-bottomed. L17–E19. *Hopper-dockers.* Shoes. E–M19. *Hopping Jesus.* A man with a limp. M19–E20.

Horn. Horn-colic. 'A temporary priapism' (*Lex.Bal.*). M18–M19. *Horny.* 'A nose; one that resounds in expectoration' (Bee). E19–E20. *Kentucky horn.* Illicit bourbon (US). M20.

Horse. 1. A lottery ticket hired for a day. M18. 2. Work charged for before completion. M18–M19. 3. A day's leave from debtors' prison. E–M19. *Die in a horse's nightcap.* Be hanged. L16–19. *Horse-breaker.* A wearer of abandoned habits (q.v.). M19. *Horse-godmother.* A large, masculine woman. M16–L19. *Horse-lop.* Plum pudding without any plums. L19. *Horse marine.* A bungling excuse for a man. (Sailors believe that the only thing more useless than an ordinary marine is one on horseback.)

M19. *Horse's leg.* A bassoon. L19–E20. *Horse's meal.* A meal without (strong) drink. L18–L19. *I work like a horse so I may as well hang my prick out to dry.* A phrase denoting apology for an accidental exposure (infrequent in polite circles). L19–M20. See also *Charley horse; City light horse; French horses, drive; Work for the dead horse.*

Horsleyism. British comstockism (q.v.). L19.

Hospital game. Rugby. L19.

Hot. Beer with gin in it. M–L19. *Hot boiler.* A stolen car (US). E–M20. *Hot coppers.* 'The feverish sensations experienced in the morning by those who have been drunk overnight' (Hotten). M–L19. *Hot-cross bun.* A Red Cross ambulance (WWI). E20. *Hot jazz.* 'Noisy dance music that blasts the ear' (Weseen) (US). E20. *Hot scone.* An Australian detective. E–M20. *Hot squat.* The electric chair (US). E–M20. *Hot-stuffer.* A habitual 'borrower' of other soldiers' kit (WWI). E20. *Hottie.* A person who is unaware that something 'humorous' has been pinned to their back. M19–20.

House. House of Commons. A privy or water closet. L18–L19. *House of noodles.* The House of Lords. E–M19.

Howdy. A midwife. 18–M20.

Howl. Howling bags. Extraordinary trousers. M–L19. *Howling cheese.* An overdressed dandy. M–L19. *Howling stick.* A flute. M–L19.

Hoxter. An inside pocket. 19.

Huey. A tramps' term for a town or village. M–L19.

Huffle. 'A piece of bestiality too filthy for explanation' (Grose). L18–E19.

Hug centre. 'Headquarters of public love-making' (Ware), e.g. a public park. L19–E20.

Hum. Hum box. A pulpit. E18–L19. *Hum cap.* Old, mellow, strong beer. L17–18. *Hum durgeon.* A dose of hypochondria, an imaginary illness. L18–L19. *Humgumptious.* Sly, deceitful. M19. *Hummer.* 1. An enormous untruth. L17–E19. 2. An impostor. M18–E19. *Hums.* Members of a church congregation. 18–E19.

Hump. 1. 'Once a fashionable word for copulation' (Grose). M–L18. 2. Ride a circus camel (US). E20. *Hump the bluey.* Travel the Australian countryside in search of employment. L19–20. *Humpy.* A primitive Australian house or hut. M–L19. See also *Hit the hump.*

Hun. 1. A German. L19–20. 2. A trainee flying officer (WW1). E20.

Hung beef. A dried bull's penis, commonly used to discipline malefactors. E19.

Hunk. A miner, particularly one of Slavic origin; more generally, an immigrant employed as a manual worker (US). L19–20.

Hunt. Hunt the dummy. Steal pocket-books. 19. *Hunt the gowk.* Play an April Fool on someone in Scotland. 18–20. *Hunt the squirrel.* A game played by coachmen in which they drive recklessly close to another carriage in order to terrify its occupants. 18–M19.

Hurrah boat. A pleasure cruiser. L19–E20.

Hurricane. An overly well-attended party at a fashionable private address. M18–E19.

Hush. Murder. 18–19. *Hush-hush.* A tank (WW1). E20.

Huzzlecoo. A flirtation (US). E20.

Hyena. A high-society heiress. L18.

Hyphenism. Divided loyalties, especially in wartime (US). E–M20.

Idiot-fringe. The hairstyle of female factory workers. L19.

Immensikoff. A thickly fur-lined overcoat. M19–E20.

Imperial pop. Ginger beer. M19.

Impudent stealing. 'Cutting out the backs of coaches, and robbing the seats' (*Lex.Bal.*). L18–M19.

Inexpressibles. Tight breeches. L18–19. (Also *Indispensables, Ineffables, Inexplicables.*)

Infanticipation. The joy of prospective parenthood (US). E20.

Ingler. A shift horse-salesman. E19–E20.

Intelligeneer. One prone to outbursts of foul language and outrageous lying when drunk. 17.

In the goslings. Adolescence (US). E–M20.

Irish. Irish apricot. A potato. L18–19. *Irish arms.* Fat legs. M18–M19. *Irish hurricane.* 'A flat calm with drizzling rain' (Bowen). M19–M20. *Irish pasture.* Unconsciousness (US). E–M20. *Weep Irish.* Volubly feign sorrow. L16–M18.

Iron. Money. L18–M19. *Ironsides.* A dancer who wears her stays on stage (US). E20. *Polish the king's iron with one's eyebrows.* Look out of a prison window. L18–M19.

Itchland. 1. Wales. L17–E18. 2. Scotland. 18–M19.

Ivy bush, like an owl in an. Said of a scrawny-faced person with big hair, or a large wig. E18–M19.

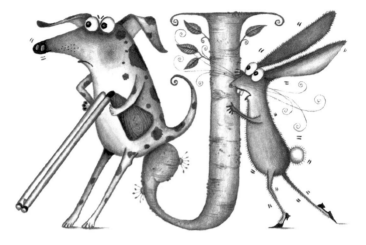

Jack. Horse-meat treated in such a way that it lacks its piquantly horsy savour. E20. *Jack at a pinch.* A stop-gap clergyman employed in an emergency. E17–19. *Jack in a box.* An unborn child, still in its mother's womb. L18–E19. *Jack Straw.* A nonentity. L16–E20. *Jack the Painter.* Powerful Australian tea. M19–20. *Jack up.* 1. Become bankrupt. L19–20. 2. Tutor someone, i.e. 'stimulate and assist' them. E–M20. *Jack whore.* 'A large, masculine, overgrown wench' (Grose). M18–M19.

Jacket. 'Remove a man by underhand and vile means from any birth or situation he enjoys' (Egan). E–M19. *Send in one's jacket.* Resign from a job. L19–E20.

Jacky. Gin. L18–E19.

Jacobite. A false shirt-front. L17–M19.

Jagger. A gentleman. M19–E20.

Jamberoo. A wild Australian party. L19–20.

Jammed. Hanged; done to death violently. E–M19.

Japan. Bread, from *du pain* (WW1). E20. *Japanned.* Be ordained as a clergyman (the black cloth of vestments resembling the colour of japan lacquer). M18–19.

Jarkman. A forger or user of false identity papers. M16–M19.

Javel. An untrustworthy individual with a taste for hanging around the docks. 18.

Jawbation. A vociferous brawl. L17–E20.

Jawkins. A club bore. M19.

Jazz. Have sex (US). L19–M20. ('If the truth were known about the origin of the word "Jazz" it would never be mentioned in polite society': *Étude*, 1924). *Jazz-baby.* A stylish and fast-living young woman (US). L19–M20. *Jazz-hound.* A philandering man. E–M20.

Jeep. A soldier's girlfriend (WWII). M20.

Jelly. An attractively curvaceous young woman. M19–E20. *Jelly-dogging.* The hunting of hares with hounds. L19.

Jemima. 1. A chamber pot. L19–E20. 2. A chambermaid. L19. *Jemimas.* Elastic-sided boots. E20.

Jemmy Squaretoes. The devil, as he is known to sailors. 19–E20.

Jerry. Jerry-diddle. A drink on the house (AUS). 20. *Jerry-wag.* A foolish young man up in town for a spree. E–M19.

Jersey hop. 'An unceremonious assembly of persons with a common taste for valsing' (Ware). L19.

Jibber the kibber. 'A method of deceiving seamen, by fixing a candle and lanthorn round the neck of a horse, one of whose fore feet is tied up; this at night has the appearance of a ship's light. Ships bearing towards it, run on shore, and being wrecked are plundered by the inhabitants. This diabolical device is, it is said, practised by the inhabitants of our western coasts' (*Lex.Bal.*). L18–E19.

Jiffess. The wife of one's employer. M–L19.

Jimbugg. A sheep (AUS: from the Aborigine for 'white mist'). M–L19. (Also *Jumbuck.*)

Jingle box. A leather drinking vessel, decorated with bells and silver trappings, used by heavy drinkers. L17–E19.

Jip. Jipper. Naval gravy. M–L19. *Jipping.* The art of dyeing part of a horse with Indian ink to conceal a flaw. M19–20.

Jitter party. 'A party of Japanese sneaking round the perimeter of a camp and trying to cause panic with strange noises and grenades' (*Forces' Slang*) (wwII). M20.

Joe. 1. A term of abuse directed at non-miners in the vicinity of a gold-field (AUS). M–L19. 2. A lavatory frequented by American students. M19–M20.

John. John Crappo. A sailor unwise enough to sport a large moustache. E–M19. *John Hall.* Alcoholic liquor (US). E–M20. *Johnny.* 1. A tiger. E–M19. 2. A penguin. L19. *Johnny-bum.* 'A he or jack ass: so-called by a lady that affected to be extremely polite and modest, who would not say jack because it was vulgar, nor ass because it was indecent' (Grose). L18–M19. *John Roberts.* The amount of alcohol required to keep a Welshman drunk while the pubs are closed on Sunday. L19. *John Thomas.* 'Generic for ... footmen with large calves and fine bushy whiskers' (Hotten). M19–E20.

Jo-jo. A disturbingly well-bearded individual (AUS). L19–E20.

Joseph. 1. A woman's great coat. L17–E19. 2. A shy young man. L17–E19.

Josser. 1. An elderly debauchee. L19. 2. A parson (AUS). L19–E20.

Jowl-sucking. Enthusiastic kissing. M–L19.

Joy-rider. 'A legless beggar who propels a low wheeled platform with his hands' (Weseen) (US). E–M20.

Juggins. Juggins-hunt. Prowl in search of someone to buy you a drink. L19. *Juggins's boy.* 'The sharp and impudent son of a stupid and easily ridiculed father' (Ware). L19.

Jumper. 1. An individual who robs houses by climbing in through the windows. L18–M19. 2. A Methodist from South Wales. L18–E19.

Jungle buzzard. A beggar who specialises in sponging or stealing off other vagrants (US). E–M20.

Juniper. Gin. 19.

Juwaubed. Have one's request for a holiday turned down by one's employer. M–L19.

Kakker-booshah. 'Accidental excrematising' (Bee). E–M19.

Kangaroo-droop. A pose in which one's hands are clasped at one's breast with the palms downwards. L19.

Karibat. Food (from Hindustani, 'curry and rice'). M19.

Katterzem. 'A man willing to go out dining at a moment's notice' (Ware). L19.

Keeping-cully. 'One who keeps a mistress, as he supposes, for his own use, but really for that of the public' (Grose). M17–M19.

Keyholed. Befuddled with alcohol (to the extent that one has difficulty unlocking one's front door). M–L19.

Kibitzer. The annoying person who stands behind one at cards and proffers uncalled-for advice. E–M20.

Kick. Kicks. Breeches. L17–E19. *Kick the gonger.* Smoke a pipe of opium (US). L19–M20. *The kick.* The apogee of fashion; cool, kickin'. L17–L19.

Kid. Kiddy. A middle-aged man who embarrassingly adopts youthful fashions. E–M19. *Kid-lay.* The art of defrauding errand boys and apprentices. L17–E19. *Kidsman.* 'One who boards and lodges boys, training them to become thieves' (Brandon). M–L19.

Kiddleywink. 1. 'A small shop where are retailed the commodities of a village store … Also, a woman of unsteady habits' (Hotten). M19–E20. 2. A West Country pub frequented by sailors. L19–20.

Kill. Kill grief. Gin. M18. (Also *Kill cobbler.*) *Kill the canary.* Skive off work. L19–E20.

Kinky. Stolen, illegally obtained (especially a car). M20.

Kirkling. The practice of robbing houses while their occupants are at church. M19.

Kit. A dancing master, or fiddler. E18–M19.

Kittle-pitchering. A humorous method of foiling a long-winded raconteur by repeatedly questioning insignificant elements of his narrative. L18–M19.

Kittly-benders. The sport of running over ice thin enough to crack under one's weight (US). M19.

Kitty hop. A proposal which exclusively benefits the person suggesting it (US). E–M20.

Kiwi king. An army officer obsessed with his soldiers' turn-out, so-called after the well-known boot polish (WWI). E20.

Knap a jacob from a dunagan-drag. The temporary theft of a night-soil-man's ladder while he is preoccupied emptying privies, in order to effect an entrance through a first-floor window: a 'curious species of robbery' (Egan). 19.

Knark. 'A hard-hearted or savage person' (Hotten). M–L19.

Knob. An officer in the Royal Navy. M17–M19.

Kokum. Specious kindness (AUS). L19.

Konoblin rig. The practice of pilfering large chunks of coal from a coal-shed. 19.

Kooferred. Killed. M19–E20.

Kraut. A morose, grumpy individual (US). 19–20.

Kriegy. A POW in Germany (WWII). M20.

Kruger's tickler. 'A little feather brush used, in the celebrations after Ladysmith and Mafeking, to tickle fellow-celebrants' faces' (Partridge). E20.

Kubber. News. M19.

Lady. Ladies of expansive sensibility. Women of pleasure. E–M19.
Lady Dacre's wine. Gin. E–M19.

Lambskin man. A judge (from his ermine trim). L17–E19.

Lame duck. A ruined stockbroker, one who doesn't honour his debts. M18–M19.

Lancepresado. One who turns up for a night out with insufficient money to pay his own way. M17–L18.

Land. Become a land-owner. Die. L19–E20. *Land-lubbers.* 'Vagabonds lurking about the country, who subsist by pilfering' (Egan). 17–E19. *Land o' Scots.* Heaven (US). L19. *Land-pirate.* A highwayman. 17–E19.

Lank sleeve. A one-armed man. L18–E19.

Lap. 'The term invariably used in the ballet girls' dressing room for gin' (Hotten). 19–E20. *Lapland.* Female society. M–L19. *Lap one's congo.* Drink tea. E19. *Lap the gutter.* Get horribly drunk. M–L19.

Lard king. An American millionaire. L19–E20.

Larry. A child's balloon with a puncture (so not very happy at all) (US). E–M20.

Lassie. A female member of the Salvation Army (US). E20.

Lassitudinarian. A congenitally lazy individual. L19–E20.

Laverick. One incapable of making a good first impression (US). L19–E20.

Lazy. Lazy-bones. A labour-saving device for fat people, allowing them to pick objects up from the ground without bending over. L18–19. *Lazy man's load.* An overly large load carried in order to avoid a second trip. L18–19.

Lech. 'A whim of the amorous kind, out of the common way' (*Lex.Bal.*). L18–19.

Leg. Break a leg. Give birth to an illegitimate child. M17–L19. *Leg-maniac.* An 'eccentric, rapid dancer' (Ware). L19–E20.

Lens louse. A moving-picture actor who somehow always manages to position himself in the foreground of every shot (US). E–M20.

Lie in state. 'Be in bed with three regular harlots' (Egan). E18–19.

Light. Light food. Tobacco chewed to assuage the appetite. L19. *Light troops.* Lice. 19. *Light wet.* Gin. E19.

Lig-robber. A thief who conceals himself under beds or inside cupboards (US). 19–20.

Lincoln's Inn. Gin. L19–20.

Lindy. Fly in an aeroplane (US). E–M20.

Links of love. Sausages (WWII). M20.

Lint-scraper. A junior surgeon. M18–L19.

Little. Little clergyman. A juvenile chimney-sweep. L18–M19. *Little mush.* A cab-driver who owns his vehicle. L19–E20. *Little snakesman.* A small boy who gains entrance to a house through the sewers in order to open the front door for his fellow thieves. L18–L19.

Liver-jerker. A tricycle. L19–E20.

Liverpool weather. Foul conditions at sea. L19–20.

Lobcock. 'A large relaxed penis' (Grose). M18–19.

Locomotive. A hot drink comprising burgundy, curaçao, egg-yolks, honey and cloves. L19–E20.

Locust. 1. Laudanum. M–L19. 2. Unspecified intoxicants, generally 'snuff and beer'. M–L19. 3. Drug a person in order to rob them. M–L19.

Lodging-slum. 'Hiring ready-furnished lodgings, and stripping them of the plate, linen, and other valuable articles' (Egan). E–M19.

Lollpoop. 'A lazy, idle drone' (B.E.). L17–18.

Lollypop joint. A rich person's residence (US). E–M20.

Long. Long attachment. A couple, comically mismatched in height, walking together. M19–20. *Long-eared chum.* A soldier's donkey (WWI). E20. (Not to be confused with his *Long-faced chum*, a horse, or his *Long-haired chum*, his girlfriend.) *Long pig.* Human flesh as food. M–L19.

Loocha. A libertine of the worst kind. 19.

Loof-faker. A chimney-sweep. M19.

Looking-glass. A chamber pot. E17–M19.

Loonslatt. A hangman's wages: thirteen and a half pence (1*s.* for labour, 1 ½*d.* for rope). L17–18.

Loose-box. 'A carriage kept for a kept woman's use' (Partridge). 19.

Lord's supper. Bread and water (US). E–M20.

Lose leather. Suffer chafing whilst riding, 'or, as the Scotch express it, to be saddle-sick' (*Lex.Bal.*). L18–E19.

Lotion. Gin. M–L19.

Loveage. Sweetened all-nations (q.v.), sold to women with a drink problem. M19.

Lullaby cheat. A baby. M18–M19.

Lully priggers. 'Thieves who steal wet linen: also, the lowest and meanest order of thieves, who go about decoying children to some bye corner, and then rob them of their clothes' (Egan). L18–L19.

Lump the lighter. Be sentenced to transportation. L18–L19.

Lunatic soup. Cheap strong drink (AUS, NZ). M20.

Lushing muzzle. A hearty slap on the chops. 19.

Lusty Lawrence. A sexual athlete. 16.

Lysken chirps. Fortune-telling by gypsies. 18–L19.

Mac. A man who consorts with prostitutes (US). L19–E20.

Macaroni-stakes. A horse race where the riders are gentlemen not professional jockeys. E19.

Mace. Obtain credit without the means to repay it. L18–E19.

Machine. Dried sheep's intestine used as a condom. 18–M19.

Mad. Mad dog. An unpaid bar bill (AUS). 20. *Mad haddock.* An idiotic or unhinged individual; an odd fish (AUS). 20. *Mad house.* An American prison with a bracingly harsh regime. E20. *Mad Mick and a banjo.* A pickaxe and shovel (AUS). E–M20. *Mad woman.* An empty carriage. E–M19.

Madam. A pocket handkerchief. M19. *Give the madam.* Answer back insolently; express oneself frankly. E–M20. *Madamoizook.* A French woman overly friendly with American soldiers (WWI). E20.

Maggies. The undergarments of Australian women. M20.

Maggot-boiler. A tallow chandler. L18–19.

Magnificents. A state of haughty indignation. E–M19.

Mags. An expected gratuity. M19.

Mahogany tree. Two parts gin to one of treacle. L18–19.

Maiden's prayer. An observation balloon (WWI). E20.

Malkintrash. Someone with appalling dress sense. L17–E19.

Maltimillionaire. A wealthy American brewer. E20.

Maltooling. Picking women's pockets on buses. M–L19.

Manany. A sailor skilled in the art of procrastination. L19–20.

Manchester. The tongue. 19.

Mandrake. A predatory homosexual. 17–E20.

Mangonise. Participate in the slave trade. 19.

Margarine mess. An early motor car. L19–E20.

Marigold. £1 million. M–L19.

Marinated. Transported as a convict. M17–M19.

Marley-stopper. An individual with astonishingly splayed feet. L19.

Marm-poosey. A flashly dressed pub landlady. M–L19.

Marriage music. The wailing of children. L17–19.

Martingale. Double one's stake after every loss. E–M19.

Martini. A demob suit (because 'straight and blue' like the rifle's barrel). E20.

Masher. A stylish and successful ladies' man. L19.

Mason. Pay for a horse with dud banknotes. M–L18.

Master of the wardrobe. An alcoholic willing to pawn his clothes for drink. L18–M19.

Matrimonial. The missionary position. M–L19.

Maw-wallop. A meal so revolting it makes one retch. L18–19.

Max. Fine gin. 19. *Maxed out.* Rip-roaringly drunk. L19.

May-gathering. Sheep-stealing. 19.

MB (or *Mark of the Beast*) *coat.* The long cassock worn by a High Churchman. M19.

Meat. Meat, drink, washing and lodging. Gin. M18. *Meaty.* Sexually desirable. 19.

Meddle class. Interfering do-gooders (US). E20.

Meemies. A state of utter hysteria (US). E–M20.

Melting moments. 'A fat man and woman in the amorous congress' (*Lex.Bal.*). 19.

Member-mug. 1. A chamber pot. L17–19. 2. A hearty, out-doorsy type of schoolboy. M19–E20.

Merry-begotten. A child born out of wedlock. L18–E19.

Mexican liniment. Petrol (US). E20.

Midshipman's watch and chain. A sheep's heart and pluck (because midshipmen would eat anything?). L18–M19.

Miffiness. A propensity to take offence. M19.

Miles's boy. Gossip; the grapevine. 19.

Milk. Milker. One who intercepts other people's telegrams. L19. *Milk the pigeon.* Attempt the impossible. M18–E20.

Milton. An oyster. M19.

Minikin. A man or woman of limited stature. L18–E19. *Tickle the minikin.* Play the lute. E–M17.

Minister's head. A boiled pig's head (US). M19–M20.

Misery. Gin. L19–E20. *Misery bowl.* 'Relief-basin – at sea' (Ware). M19–E20.

Misleading paper. The Times of London. L19–E20.

Mocteroof. Disguise the blemishes in fruit and vegetables in order to get a better price at market. M–L19.

Mofussilite. A countrified inhabitant of a rural district, a hayseed. M–L19.

Mohair. A scornful soldiers' term for a civilian. L18–M19.

Mohican. 'A very heavy man that rides a long way in an omnibus for sixpence' (Partridge). M19.

Moko. A pheasant 'accidentally' shot before the start of the season. M–L19.

Moll. Moll-sack. A handbag. M19. *Moll Thompson's mark,* i.e. MT (empty). L18–L19.

Molly. Miss Molly. An effeminate man, or homosexual. M18–L19. *Mollydooker.* A left-handed Australian. M20.

Molocker. A reconditioned hat. M–L19.

Momblishness. Muttering (US). E20.

Monday mice. The noticeable number of black eyes to be seen after the weekend's excesses. L19–20.

Moneymoon. A gold-digger's honeymoon (US). E20.

Monkey. Have a monkey up the chimney. Take out a mortgage on one's house. L19. *Monkey-dodger.* An Australian sheep-hand. E20. *Monkey on a gridiron.* A cyclist. L19–E20. *Monkey's parade.* A street where men and women go to pick up members of the opposite sex. L19–E20. *Pickled monkey.* 'A species of animal served by the Germans to prisoners of war as food. Its identity was never determined' (*War Slang*) (WWI). E20. *Stuffed monkey.* 'A very pleasant close almond biscuit' (Ware). M19–E20. *Where the monkey sleeps.* 19. See *Monosyllable*. See also *High monkey-monk*; *Suck the monkey*.

Monosyllable. 'A woman's commodity' (*Lex.Bal.*). E18–L19.

Monowongler. An American who entirely monopolises the conversation. E20.

Montygram. A signal written personally by Field Marshal Montgomery (WWII). M20.

Mooch. Sponge off one's friends. M19–E20.

Moon. Moon-eyed hen. A woman with an unfortunate squint. L18–L19. *Moon-man.* A gypsy. 17–E19. *Moon-raker.* An inhabitant of Wiltshire, 'because it is said that some men of that county, seeing the reflection of the moon in a pond, endeavoured to pull it out with a rake' (*Lex.Bal.*). M18–E19. *Moonshine.* 1. Smuggled white brandy or gin. L18–L19. 2. Rice (US). E20.

Mophy. A dainty young man who pays great attention to his personal grooming. L19–20.

Morocco man. A fraudulent insurance salesman. L18–M19.

Mort wap-apace. A sexually experienced or proficient woman, a good lay. L18–E19.

Mosh. Dine at a restaurant and leave without paying. 19–E20.

Mother. Mother's blessing. Laudanum (i.e. brandy and opium) dispensed to overexcited children. M–L19. *Mother's milk.* Gin. E19. (Also *Mother's ruin.* L19–M20.)

Mouse. 1. A woman arrested for brawling in the street. L16–L18. 2. A man incapable of consummating his marriage on his wedding night. 19. *Speak like a mouse in a cheese,* i.e. in a muffled or indistinct manner, faintly. L16–E20. See also *Monday mice.*

Moustachitis. An obsession with cultivating moustaches (US). E20.

Move the laundry. Smuggle Chinese illegal immigrants into the USA. E20.

Mrs Jones. A water closet. M–L19.

Mud-kicker. A woman who picks up a man in order to rob him (US). E20.

Muffin-faced. Possessing an oddly bulging visage. E–M19.

Muggle party. A casual get-together of American girls. E20.

Mugwump. An impotent man. M19.

Mulga madness. A type of personality disorder, common among poons (q.v.), caused by spending too much time in one's own company (AUS). 19.

Mulligatawney. 'Soup made of unborn calves' meat and still-born *foetae*, in imitation of the Chinese "*chow, chow*" or stewed puppy-dogs' (Bee). E–M20.

Mulligrubs. A state of depression. 17–M20.

Mullock over. Shear sheep in a slapdash manner (AUS). L19.

Mumper. A genteel beggar. L17–E19.

Mundungus. 'Bad or rank tobacco: from *mondongo*, a Spanish word signifying tripes, or the uncleaned entrails of a beast, full of filth' (*Lex.Bal.*). M17–E19.

Museum headache. The irritable boredom caused by having to wait for one's books in the Reading Room of the British Library (once part of the British Museum). M19–E20.

Mushroom-faker. An itinerant umbrella-maker. M19.

Musical soup-eater. A coarse, vulgar individual (US). E20.

Muskin, unaccountable. An ineffable eccentric. M18.

Mustard shine. The application of mustard-oil to one's shoes to throw bloodhounds off the scent (US). E20.

Mutton. Mutton-monger. An incorrigible womaniser. M16–M19. *Mutton-shunter.* A policeman. L19–E20. *Mutton-thumper.* An incompetent workman. L18–E20.

Muzzle. 'A beard, (usually) long and nasty' (B.E.). L17–M19.

Mystery. A sausage. L19.

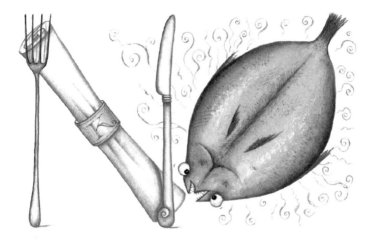

Nab the teaze. Be whipped, privately. L18–M19.

Nacky. Ingenious. L18–E19.

Naggle. Hold one's nose in the air in a haughtily affected manner. M19–E20.

Nana. Shockingly indecent. L19. *Nana cut.* A brutal short-back-and-sides (AUS). M20.

Nanny-house. A brothel. L17–19.

Nantee-narking. Enormous fun. E–M19.

Nap. A strikingly pointed moustache. M19. *Napper of naps.* A sheep-stealer. L17–18.

Nappy. Used to describe a recalcitrant horse with a mind of its own. M19–E20.

Narrative. The tail of a dog. E19.

Nasty man. The person in a gang of stranglers who does the actual garrotting. M19.

Natty lad. A child thief or pickpocket. L18–M19.

Navigator. A potato. M19.

Neardy. A figure of authority: a parent, employer, etc. M–L19.

Nebuchadnezzar. 1. The penis. M19–E20. 2. A vegetarian. M19–E20. (See Daniel 4:32–3.)

Necking. The practice of tying a disruptive cow to a more placid animal (US). E20.

Neddy. 1. A small cosh, or life-preserver. M19. 2. A large amount of something. M19.

Neecee peeress. A woman of no family but immense fortune who is married to a penniless aristocrat. L19–E20.

Needle. Needle and pin. Gin. L19–20. *Needle beer.* Beer spiked with neat alcohol or ether (US). E–M20.

Needy-mizzler. A down-at-heel-looking individual. E–M19.

Nervous pudding. A dessert made with gelatin (US). M20.

Nestor. A diminutive public-schoolboy. M–L19.

Never. Never-never land. The outback (AUS). M19–E20. *Never-squedge.* 'A poor, pulseless, passionate youth' (Ware). L19–E20.

New. New light. A Methodist. L18–E19. 2. An individual who helps criminals escape from prison. M19. *The new drop.* 'The scaffold used at Newgate for hanging criminals; which dropping down, leaves them suspended. By this improvement the use of that vulgar vehicle, a cart, is entirely left off' (*Lex.Bal.*). L18–M19.

Newcastle hospitality. An attempt to kill a person with kindness. M19–E20.

Newgate knocker. A long, greasy love-lock. M19.

Nibble. 'Pilfer trifling articles, not having spirit to touch any thing of consequence' (Egan). E19–20.

Nicker. A young man who obtains his entertainment by breaking windows with coins of low denomination. E18.

Nicknackatory. A place selling baubles, gadgets and curiosities; a gift shop. L18–E19.

Niffynaffy fellow. A trifler, a waste of space. L18–E19.

Niggle. 'Have to do with a woman carnally' (Harman). M16–E19.

Night-hawk. A London prostitute. M–L19.

Nimgimmer. A medical practitioner, particularly one specialising in venereal complaints. L17–E19.

Nincumpoop. A fool: 'one who never saw his wife's ——' (Grose). L17–20.

90 dog. A pug (from the jaunty curl to its tail). L19–E20.

Nipple chaser. An oilrig foreman (US). E20.

Nit. 'Wine that is brisk, and poured quick into a glass' (B.E.), i.e. sparkling wine. L17–M18.

Nixie. An undeliverable letter or package (US). E20.

Nocky boy. A simpleton. L18–E19.

Noffgur. A modish prostitute. L19–E20.

Noisy-dog racket. The practice of stealing brass door-knockers. E–M19.

Nonsense. 'Melted butter in a wig' (*Lex.Bal.*). L18–E19.

No rats. A Scotsman (from the well-known aversion of rodents to bagpipe music). M19–E20.

North. North Country compliment. 'To give or offer anything that is not wanted by either giver or receiver' (Hotten). M–L19. *North-easter.* A sailor whose pay-packet is much smaller than he was expecting (i.e. bitter). L19–20. *North Sea pheasant.* A kipper. L19–E20.

Norway neckcloth. A pillory, because often made of Norway fir. L18–M19.

Norwicher. A drinker who helps himself to more than his fair share from a communal tankard or bottle. M–L19.

Nose. Nose and chin. Gin. L18–E19. *Nose-bag show.* The entertainment derived from watching someone eat their lunch out of a paper bag (US). E20.

Notergal wash. Obviously grubby (perhaps from Florence Nightingale's belief that one could keep perfectly clean on a pint of water a day). M–L19.

Nubbly. Smutty. L19–E20.

Nugging-dress. An exotic or unusual gown, especially a loose one as favoured by prostitutes. L17–M19.

Nuisanship. The noble art of making oneself obnoxious to others (US). E20.

Nursing. The theft of another bus company's passengers. 19.

Nut. 'Please a person by any little act of assiduity, by a present, or by flattering words' (Egan). 19.

Oat. Oatmeal party. An agglomeration of Scotsmen. 19. *Oatsmobile.* A horse (US). E20.

Obliquitous. 'Oblivious of distinction between right and wrong' (Hotten). M19.

Oil. Anoint with the oil of gladness. Administer a thrashing. L18–E19. *Oil dorado.* A land of black gold: a territory with rich oil reserves (US). E20. *Oiligarchy.* Rich and powerful members of the oil interest (US). E–M20. *Oil of angels.* Money used as a bribe. 17. *Oil of barley.* Strong beer. M17–E19. *Oily rag.* A cigarette (rhyming slang rather than referring to the aftertaste). E–M20.

Old. Old bendy. The devil. 18–19. *Old fogey.* An invalid soldier. L18–M19. *Old folks.* Circus chimps (US). E20. *Old gown.* Contraband tea. M19. *Old Harry.* 'A composition used by vintners when they bedevil their wines' (B.E.). L17–E19. *Old hat.* The female genitalia (because 'frequently felt'). L17–L19. *Old horse.* Salt meat well past its best-before date. M19. *Old lag.* A transported convict who returns to Britain. M–L19. *Old pegg.* An unpleasant, low-fat Yorkshire cheese. 18–M19. *Old smoky.* The electric chair (US). M20. *Old Tom.* Potent gin. E19–M20.

Oliver. A fist. M19–M20. *Oliver's skull.* A chamber pot (in contemptuous allusion to Cromwell). L17–M19. *Oliver whiddles.* The moon shines. L18–M19.

Ollapod. A country chemist. M19.

One. One-bite. A wincingly sour apple. M–L19. *One in ten.* A parson (in reference to his tithes). L17–19.

Onion hunters. 'A class of young thieves who are on the look out for gentlemen who wear their seals suspended on a ribbon, which they cut, and thus secure the seals or other trinkets suspended to the watch' (*Lex.Bal.*). E–M19.

Oofless. The state of temporary financial embarrassment. L19.

Oozipootics or *Ooperzootics.* A minor undiagnosed malady or worrying little hypochondriacal niggle. L19.

Oozy. An elephant operator (WWII). M20.

Orchestras, the. Testicles (rhyming slang, *Orchestra stalls*). L19–20.

Ornithorhynchus. An Australian creditor (i.e. a 'beast with a bill'). L19–E20.

Orthodoxy and heterodoxy. 'Somebody explained these terms by saying, the first was a man who had a doxy of his own, the second a man who made use of the doxy of another man' (*Lex.Bal.*). E19.

Oscar. 1. A male homosexual. L19–E20. 2. Money. E–M20.

Ottomise. Dissect. M18–M19.

Out. Out and out kicksies builder. A superlative trouser-maker. M19. *Out of print.* A booksellers' description for someone deceased. E–M19. *Out on the pickaroon.* Ready for anything; up for it. M19. *Outrun the constable.* Live beyond one's means. M18–E19.

Overseer. A man in the pillory. M18–E19.

Owler. A nocturnal cross-Channel wool-smuggler. L17–E19.

Oyster. A gobbet of thick phlegm. L18–20. *Cincinatti oyster.* A pickled pig's foot. E–M20. *Oysterics.* The health scare caused by a spate of food-poisonings attributed to eating bad oysters. E20.

Pabunuf. A worthless individual, or bad egg (*pas bon œuf*) (US). E20.

Pad. 1. A highway. M16–19. 2. A highway robber. M17–M19. *Pad-nag.* An easy-going horse. M17–E19.

Paddington spectacles. The hood pulled over a condemned man's head prior to hanging. L18–E19.

Paddy. Do Paddy Doyle. Spend time as a defaulter in an army cell. L19–M20. *Paddy-melon.* A diminutive kangaroo (AUS). M19–20. *Paddy whack.* A well-built Irishman. 18–E19.

Page Mark Twain. Imagine what Mark Twain would have done in order to guide one's own conduct (cf. today's 'WWJD?') (US). E20.

Pain in the puku. A stomach ache (NZ). 20.

Palliard. A clapperdogeon (q.v.) who excites charity by affecting revolting sores. L15–L18.

Palpitate with actuality. Blindingly obvious. L19.

Panny. A violent tussle between two or more women. L19.

Panshite. Absolutely petrified. L19–E20.

Pantiler. A religious prisoner. E19.

Pants. A man (US). M20.

Panupetaston. A large, ill-fitting student overcoat. M19.

Panzer Pete. 'A liquor made by troops in New Guinea. Ingredients: four tins of apricots, four dessertspoonsful of yeast, 5 lbs. sugar, four handsful of sultanas, 3 gals. water. Stand for six days' (Baker, Aus.). M20.

Panzy. A burglary. M–L19.

Par-banging. Walking the streets to find employment. L19.

Parlezvoo lingo. French. M18–E19.

Parlour snake. A male student who loiters round female undergraduates with intent (US). E20.

Parson. A road sign (see *Finger-post*). M–L18.

Pateepan. A small pie. L17–E18.

Patricoes or *Pater-coves.* 'Strolling priests that marry under a hedge without gospel or common-prayer book, the couple standing on each side [of] a dead beast, are bid to live together till death them do part, so shaking hands, the wedding is ended' (B.E.). 16–L18.

Paup along. (Of the upper and middle classes) struggle courageously to make ends meet. L19–E20.

Pawnee-game. The drinking of water instead of alcohol. L19.

Pay away. Eat voraciously. L18–M20.

Peach. 'An informer against omnibus conductors and drivers' (Hotten); an undercover ticket inspector. M19.

Peacock. 1. Pay a morning visit on one's female acquaintance in expectation of receiving beer as refreshment. M–L19. 2. Cherry-pick the best tracts of land for purchase (AUS). L19.

Pearl-diver. A kitchen worker employed to wash dishes (US). E–M20.

Pear-making. 'Taking bounties from several regiments and immediately deserting' (*Lex.Bal.*). E–M19.

Peas. Sexually aroused (*peas in the pot*, hot). L19–E20.

Peat man. An incompetent safe-cracker (US). E20.

Peculiar. 1. A mistress. L17–19. 2. An evangelical churchman. M19.

Pedlar. Pedlar's French. Canting slang. M16–19. *Pedlar's pony.* A walking stick. L18–19.

Peewee soft-song man. A small-scale con-artist (US). E20.

Peg a hack. 'To mount the box of a hackney-coach, drive yourself, and give the jarvey a holiday' (Egan). E–M19.

Penguin. The man who disposes of the earth from an escape tunnel in a prisoner-of-war camp (WWII). M20.

Pennsylvania hurricane. A swingeing untruth (US). E20.

Penny. Penny death-trap. A cheap paraffin lamp, especially one made in Germany. L19–E20. *Pennyweight job.* A jewel robbery, from a unit of measure for gems (US). E20. *Penny-white.* Said of one whose wealth more than makes up for their physical imperfections. 17–18.

Pensioner. 'A man of the most degraded condition who lives off the miserable earnings of a prostitute. There is an unmentionable prefix to the word *Pensioner*' (Hotten). 19. In some authorities the unprintable epithet is: *petticoat.*

Pepper-proof. Uninfected by venereal disease. L17–18.

Peptimist. An ebullient individual (US). E20.

Perishable cargo. Either fruit or slaves. M–L18.

Peristaltic persuaders. 'Dr Kitchener's relief balls for gourmands' (Bee). E–M19.

Perpendicular. 1. A buffet lunch with insufficient seating. M19. 2. Sex while standing up. M19–20.

Perpetual pest. A Ford motor car. E20.

Persuaders. Spurs. L18–E19.

Peter. Peter-hunting. Prowling the highways in search of trunks and cases to steal from the backs of stagecoaches. 19. *Peterman.* One who employs 'unlawful engines' to catch fish in the Thames. L17–E18. See also *Panzer Pete.*

Pettyfogger. An unscrupulous but inadequate back-street lawyer. 16–19.

Pharaoh. Strong beer. L17–E19.

Philander. 'To ramble on incoherently; to write discursively and weakly' (Hotten). M19–E20.

Philistines. Earwigs or other such insects. L17–20.

Phiz-gig. Mutton dressed as lamb. 19.

Pianocracy. The collective noun for a herd of pianists (US). E20.

Piccadilly. Piccadilly bushman. A wealthy Australian living in London. E–M20. *Piccadilly weepers.* Long, carefully combed-out side-whiskers. M–L19. *Piccadilly window.* A monocle. L19–E20.

Pickaxe. A stimulating tipple favoured by South African diamond-miners: rough whisky or brandy and pontac wine, cut with ginger beer. L19.

Pickle. Pickle-manufacturer. A publisher of badly produced, poor-quality books. L19–E20. *Pickling-tubs.* Wellington boots. M19.

Picnic. An unpleasant experience (AUS). L19–20.

Pig. A police officer. E19–20. *Give cold pig.* Wake someone by dousing with cold water or stripping off the bedclothes. M18–L19. *Keep a pig.* Have a student lodger or room-mate. M19–E20. *Pig between sheets.* A ham sandwich (US). E20. *Pig-islander.* An inhabitant of New Zealand (AUS, NZ). L19–20. *Pig-skin artist.* An Australian jockey. M20. *Pig-wam.* An American pigsty. E20. *Pig-widgeon.* A fool, or muppet. L17–L19.

Pillow-puncher. A chambermaid in an American hotel. 20.

Pills. Testicles (from the famous Beecham's Pills, which claimed always to 'get results'). M20.

Pilot. The name for a blind beggar's guide dog (US). E20.

Pimginnit. 'A large, red, angry pimple' (B.E.). L17–18.

Pimp. A fire-lighter. 18. *Pimp stick.* A roll-up cigarette (US). M20. *Pimp whiskin.* A pre-eminent pimp. M17–E19.

Pin-basket. The youngest child in a family. 18–M19.

Ping. Speak quickly in a ringing high-pitched voice. E–M19.

Pinking-dindee. An Irishman who randomly assaults passers-by for pleasure. M–L18.

Pintle. Pintle-de-pantledy. Scared silly. M17–E19. *Pintle-keek.* A come-hither look attempted by a Scotsman. 19–E20. *Pintle-smith.* A surgeon. L18–E20.

Pip-squeak. A shell fired from a light gun (WWI). E20.

Piss. Piss down someone's back. Flatter them. L18–19. *Piss-proud.* Possess 'a false erection' (*Lex.Bal.*). L18–20. *Piss-quick.* Gin and hot water spiked with marmalade. M19. *Piss when one can't whistle.* Be hanged. L18–E19.

Placer. A sheep with a strong attachment to a particular location (AUS). L19–20.

Play. *Play at pully hauly.* Have sexual intercourse. L18–E20. *Play booty.* Deliberately throw a game or race. E16–E19. *Play pussy.* 'Speed from one cloud to another in order to escape detection or to pounce upon a shadowed enemy aircraft' (*Forces' Slang*) (WWII). M20. *Play the corker.* Irritate those around one. L19–E20. *Play the piano.* Drop bombs one at a time from a plane (WWII). M20. *Play with the squirrels.* Take up residence in an asylum (US). E20.

Pleep. A cowardly Luftwaffe pilot (WWII). M20.

Pling. Beg on the street (US). E20.

Plink plonk. White wine (i.e. *vin blanc*) (WWI). E20.

Plump. *Plump his peepers.* Bestow a pair of black eyes. L18–M19. *Plumpers.* 'Contrivances said to be formerly worn by old maids, for filling out a pair of shrivelled cheeks' (Grose). 18.

Plum-pudding. A spotted dog which runs after carriages. M19.

Pneumatic cavalry. Soldiers equipped with bicycles. E–M20.

Poddy-dodging. The theft of calves before they are old enough to be branded (AUS). E–M20.

Poet lariat. A cowboy poet (US). E20.

Poggled. Disconcerting, because mad or drunk; also, disconcerted (WWI). E20.

Pogram. A Nonconformist. M–L19.

Pogy. Inebriated. L18–L19.

Poison-pate. One who suffers the indignity of red hair. L17–M19.

Poke-pudding or *Pock-pud.* A Scots name for an Englishman. E18–L19.

Pollrumptious. Bursting with misguided confidence. M–L19.

Pomegranate. A Briton who goes to live in Australia (i.e. pommie + immigrant). E20.

Ponce. 1. 'A degraded man who lives upon a woman's prostitution. Low-class East-end thieves even will "draw the line" at *Ponces*, and object to their presence in the boozing-kens' (Hotten). L19. 2. A toy boy (US). E20.

Pong. 1. Beer. M–L19. 2. Turn somersaults. M19–20.

Pontius Pilate. 1. A pawnbroker. L18–19. 2. 'A Mr Shepherd, of Trinity College [Cambridge]; who disputing with a brother parson on the comparative rapidity with which they read the liturgy, offered to give him as far as Pontius Pilate in the Belief' (*Lex.Bal.*). E19.

Poodle. Poodle-faker. An army or naval officer over-dedicated to his social life; a social climber. E20. *The Poodle.* The English Channel. L19–20.

Pooh-gaciss. A South African expression of disgust. L19–E20.

Poon. An unstable solitary dweller in the Australian outback. M20.

Poor. Poor-creatures. A contemptuous term for 'the prince of esculents', the potato. E–M19. *Poor man's side.* South London. L19.

Poperine pear. A man's penis. L16–M17.

Pop one's tatler. Pawn one's watch. M18–19.

Poppy-show. An accidental flaunting of one's underwear before the public gaze. L19–M20.

Porridge-disturber. An unpleasantly hard punch in the stomach. E–M19.

Portuguese. 'The old Navy name for all foreigners except Frenchmen' (Bowen). L19. *Portuguese pumping.* 'Ask sailors the meaning of this phrase, and they may laugh a good deal, but they give no etymology. It is probably nasty' (Ware). L19–E20.

Possess good understandings. Own exceptionally big boots. M–L19.

Postcardy. Unsophisticated and unpolished (US). E20.

Potching. A practice of amoral waiters: the accepting of tips from customers they have not served. L19.

Pot-wabbler. An individual who fulfils the criteria in some boroughs of being a householder, thereby entitling him to vote in parliamentary elections. L18–E19.

Poulterer. A thief who steals letters in order to rob them of their contents. 19.

Poverty. Gin. M18. (Also *Royal poverty.* M–L18.)

Powder-wagon. A sawn-off shotgun (US). E20.

Pozzy-wallah. A soldier addicted to jam (WWI). E20.

Prattling-box. A pulpit. L18–M19.

Pratts. The buttocks. M16–20.

Pray with one's knees upwards. 'Said of a woman much given to gallantry and intrigue' (Grose). L18–E19.

Pretty-boy clip. A pudding-bowl or page-boy fringe. L19.

Prick. An irritatingly cheeky boy or teenager. M16. *Prick-eared.* Possess ears longer than one's hair. M–L17.

Prig-napper. A thief-taker. L17–E19. *Prig-star.* A competitor for another's affections. M17–18.

Privateer. A part-time prostitute, one not wholly reliant on the trade for her livelihood. L19–E20.

Prognostic. A gourmet (literally 'one who knows his food'). E20.

Prohibishop. A cleric opposed to selling alcohol (US). E20.

Prosser. An idle, loafing sponger. M–L19.

Psalm-smiter. An overenthusiastic evangelical; a very happy clappy. M19.

Public ledger. 'A prostitute: because, like that paper, she is open to all parties' (*Lex.Bal.*). L18–19.

Pudden. Drug a dog in order to rob a house without being disturbed. M19.

Pukaroo. Mess something up (NZ). L19–20.

Pull-down. A long droopy moustache (successor to the nap, q.v.). L19.

Pump-thunder. A loud-mouthed blagueur. 19.

Pum-pum. A violin player. 18–M19.

Punchable nun. A prostitute. E18.

Pung. Fall asleep while on duty at the telephone (WWI). E20.

Punk. 1. 'A little whore' (B.E.). L16–E20. 2. A punctured bicycle tyre. L19–20. 3. A lion cub, or other juvenile circus animal (US). E20. *Punk and plaster.* Bread and butter (US). 19–20.

Puppy's mama. 'A jocular way of calling a woman a bitch' (*Lex.Bal.*). L18–M19.

Purby. A Pre-Raphaelite. L19.

Pure. Pure-finder. A street-cleaner responsible for picking up dogs' mess. M19–E20. *Pure Merino.* A self-important member of a distinguished Australian family, or one without convict origins. 19.

Purl. Hot porter infused with wormwood and served with a dash of gin as an early-morning winter warmer. L17–E20.

Purple. Purple dromedary. 'A bungler in the art and mystery of thieving' (Grose). L17–18. *Purple passion.* The object of undisclosed affections (US). E20.

Pussy. Pussy-cat. A very High Church, 'bells and smells' Anglican (i.e. a Puseyite). M19. *Pussy-foot.* Sidle up to someone tentatively with the aim of asking them out (US). E20.

Put. Put on a boss. Adopt a baleful expression. L19–E20. *Put on big pants.* Act a cowboy role in a film or play (US). E20. *Put one under the oxygen tent.* Break off a relationship (US). E20. *Put the bee on.* Con someone, usually by means of a hard-luck story, i.e. sting them (US). E–M20.

Putty-cove. An unreliable person, one lacking backbone. 19.

Puzzling-sticks. The triangular frame to which malefactors are tied in order to be flogged. E–M19.

Pyjamas. Pyjamazon. A statuesque woman attired for bed (US). E20. *Pyjamorino.* A parade of pyjama-clad students (US). E20.

Quack. Publish a book under a misleading new title. 17–20. *Quacking-cheat.* A duck. M16–M19.

Qually. (Of wine) 'turbulent and foul' (B.E.). L17–M18.

Quandary. 'One so over-gorged as to be doubtful which he should do first, shite or spew' (Grose). M16–19.

Quarrel-picker. A glazier. 17–18.

Queer. A dealer in inferior soot-substitutes. E–M19. *Queer bird.* A criminal released from prison who returns to his wicked ways. M16–E19. *Queer bluffer.* The landlord of a public house frequented by thieves, fraudsters and cut-throats. L17–M19. *Queer fella.* A commanding officer (WWI). E20. *Queer kicks.* Substandard trousering. L17–E19. *Queer prancer.* A timorous horse-thief. L18–E19. *Queer rooster.* An informer who pretends sleep in order to eavesdrop on the conversations of criminals. L18–L19.

Quibberdick. A tiresomely argumentative American. E20.

Quiff the bladder. Hide one's baldness; sport a comb-over. L19. See also *Bladder of lard.*

Quinky. Apprehensive, jittery (US). E20.

Quockerwodger. A puppet on a string; hence, a politician in thrall to big business or other interest-groups. M19.

Quoob. A square fish in a round hole, a misfit (US). E20.

Rabbit. Rabbit-catcher. A midwife. L18–M19. *Rabbit-pie shifter.* A policeman. M19–E20. *Rabbit suckers.* Feckless young spendthrifts who pay over the odds while running up vast debts. *Run the rabbit.* Pick up some beer from the off-licence (AUS). L19. See also *Dead rabbit; Welsh rabbit.*

Rachel. Rejuvenate (after a beautician who lied about the benefits of her products). L19.

Raffle-coffin. A body-snatcher. 19.

Rag. Rag-sooker. An ingenious instrument for removing clothes-pegs so that linen can be removed nefariously from washing lines at long distance. L19. *Rag-time.* Any military display of ridiculous inefficiency (WWI). E20. *Rag-water.* Gin, or some other cheap spirit. L17–M19.

Railroad Bible. A deck of cards (US). L19.

Rainbow. A recruit who arrives just after the end of a battle (WWI). E20.

Ram. Ram-cat. A man bedizened in furs. M–L19. *Ram-reel.* An all-male dance. 19.

Ramfeezled. Exhausted. L19–E20.

Randle. Punish a boy for farting. 19.

Rank. Rank bounce. A stylishly dressed or well-turned-out individual. L18–E19. *Rank rider.* A highwayman. L17–E18.

Rantallion. 'One whose scrotum is so relaxed as to be longer than his penis' (Grose). L18–M19.

Rapper. A witness in a criminal trial (US). L18–E20.

Rascal. 'A man without genitals' (Grose). M18–M19.

Rasher of wind. An especially thin individual. M19–E20.

Rational costume. The female trouser. L19.

Rattling mumper. A beggar who pesters coaches. M17–E19.

Rave. An unrequited passion, a crush. E20.

Raven. A minuscule portion of pub bread and cheese. L19.

Razzle-dazzlers. Lurid socks. L19.

Red. Red cross. Morphine (US). M20. *Red eye.* A fried egg (US). E–M20. *Red lead.* Tomato ketchup (US). M20. *Red neck.* A Roman Catholic in the north of England. 19. *Red tape.* Brandy. L18–E19. *Red-underwear type.* An old-fashioned person (US). E20.

Reefer. A refrigerated railway wagon (US). E20.

Releasing officer. One's father (because he pays one's debts). M–L19.

Religious painter. A painfully bad artist, i.e. 'one who does not break the commandment which prohibits the making of the likeness of any thing in heaven or earth' (*Lex.Bal.*). L18–E19.

Republic of letters. The post office. M19.

Re-raw, on the. A wild night out; on the lash. M–L19.

Rest camp. A cemetery (WWI). E20.

Reversed. Turned upside down by thieves so that the money falls out of one's pockets. L17–18.

Rhino. 1. Money. L17–L19. 2. A condition of depression or despondency experienced by American sailors. E20.

Rhubarb. An advance on one's wages. L19–E20.

Ribbon. Gin. L18–M19.

Rice Christians. 'People who make of religion a business' (Ware). L19–E20.

Ride. Ride in old boots. Inherit someone else's mistress. L18–M19. *Ride rusty.* Sulk. L18–M19. *Ride St George.* Sexual intercourse with the woman on top. 'This is said to be the way to get a bishop' (*Lex.Bal.*). L17–M19. *Ride to Rumford.* Treat oneself to a new pair of leather breeches, or have the seat of an old pair 'new bottomed'. L18–E19.

Right nanty. Gin. M18. (Also *Right sort.* M19.)

Ringer. The fastest sheep-shearer in a shed (AUS, NZ). 19–20.

Ritualistic knee. Repetitive strain injury caused by excessive devotional kneeling among poorly trained Anglicans. M19.

Rizzle. Relish a brief period of peaceful post-prandial contemplation. L19.

Roaring. Roaring boy. A riotous, noisy individual. E17–M18. *Roaring horn.* An urgent erection (AUS). L19–20.

Roast. Tap out a telegraph message too quickly for it to be followed. L19.

Roger. 1. A beggar who disguises himself as a university student. M16. 2. A suitcase. L17–E19.

Roll me in the kennel. Gin. M18.

Romboyled. Wanted by the police. L17–E19.

Rome. Rome mort. Queen Elizabeth I. M16–E17. *Rome-ville.* London. 16–17.

Root. Root-about. 'Promiscuous football practice' (Partridge). L19–20. *Rooty.* Soldiers' term for bread, or rum. 19.

Ropper. A scarf. L19.

Rork. A non-public-schoolboy. L19.

Rortyness. Vigorous vitality. L19.

Roscoe. A revolver (US). L19–E20.

Rotten-logging. Foreplay (US). E20.

Royal scamp. A highwayman with perfect manners, who remembers his manners when conducting his trade. L18–E19.

Rubber. Rubber gun. A heavy piece of artillery fired at maximum range (WWI). E20. *Rubber mule.* A circus elephant (US). E20. *Rubberneck wagon.* A vehicle occupied by sightseers (US). L19–20.

Ruffin. 1. The devil. M16–E19. 2. A Justice of the Peace. E17–E19.

Ruffmans. Woods, or thick undergrowth. E17–M19.

Ruggins. Bed. E–M19.

Ruin. Gin. E–M19.

Rum. 1. A term of strong approbation. M17–19. 2. An impecunious rural clergyman in Ireland. E–M18. *Rum bubber.* A thief skilled at stealing silver tankards from public houses. L17–18. *Rum chub.* 'Among butchers, a customer easily imposed on, as to the quality and price of meat' (Grose). L17–E19. *Rum dubber.* A skilled lock-picker. 17–18. *Rum fuddle.* An excellent drink. 17–18. *Rum gutlers.* Sweet wine from the Canary Islands. M17–18. *Rum kicks.* Flash pants; gold or silver brocade breeches. L17–E19. *Rum mawnd.* An impersonator of idiots. L17–18. *Rum strum.* A fine, flowing wig. L17–18.

Rumbler's flunkey. A person who fetches cabs in return for a tip; a footman. 19.

Rumbusticator. A financially well-endowed man. L19–E20.

Rump. Rump-and-kidney men. 'Fiddlers that play at feasts, fairs, weddings, etc. and live chiefly on the remnants' (B.E.). L17–E19. *Rumping.* The practice of pointedly turning one's back on an acquaintance. E20.

Rumtitum. In fine fettle. E–M19.

Run. Running smobble. The practice of snatching items from a shop counter and throwing them to an accomplice who makes a speedy getaway. L18–M19. *Run through the nose with a cushion.* Smack someone in a jocular manner. L17–E18. *Run to seed.* Pregnant. M19. See also *Rabbit, run the.*

Runt. A mature canary. L17.

Rushers. 'Thieves who knock at the doors of great houses, in London, in summer time, when the families are out of town, and on being opened by a woman, rush in and rob the house' (Grose). L18–M19.

Rusty guts. A surly, antisocial individual. L17–M18.

Sacking law. The oldest profession. 16–E17.

Sad cattle. 1. 'Impudent, lewd women' (B.E.). L17–18. 2. Gypsies. 18–E19.

Saddle. Saddle the spit. Give a dinner. L18–M19. *Saddling paddock.* 'Any favourite open-air place for amorous assignations' (*Slang*) (AUS). E–M20.

Sailor. A soldier both willing and able to buy his friends drinks. M19–E20.

Saint. St Geoffrey's Day. 'Never, there being no saint of that name' (*Lex.Bal.*). L18–M19. *St Giles's Greek.* Thieves' cant. E17–19. *St Louis flats.* A jazz man's shoes (US). E–M20. *St Lubbock's Day.* August bank holiday (after the institution's initiator). L19–E20. See also *Ride St George.*

Salad. An enjoyable snooze after being woken for the first time. L19. *Salad march.* A parade of ballet girls. L19–E20.

Salamander. A fire-eating street performer. M19.

Salisbury. A white lie or civil evasion. L19.

Sal slappers. A woman with very healthy appetites. L19.

Salt-boxes. The condemned cells at Newgate prison. 19.

Sam. 1. A Liverpudlian. M19. 2. A fool. M19.

Sammy-house. A Hindu temple (from Sankrit *suamin*, 'lord').
M–L19.

Sanakatowzer. A sockdolager (q.v.).

San Fairy Ann. A phrase expressive of British soldiers' phlegmatism; who cares? (wwi). E20.

Sangaree. A heavy drinking bout, a binge (from *sangria*). E–M19.

Sangster. An umbrella. M19.

Sappodil. A mild-mannered and trusting fellow; a sucker (US). E20.

Sap-sucker. An extortionist (US). E20.

Satchel-arsed fellow. A wearer of ill-fitting trousers. 19.

Satin. Gin. M19–M20.

Satyr. A hardened horse-, cattle- or sheep-rustler. E18.

Savage. An overenthusiastic American policeman. E–M20.

Saving chin. A long pointy chin (cf. e.g. 'He's so mean he would save the droppings from his nose'). L18–M19.

Sawney-hunter. A desperate bacon- and cheese-thief. M19.

Scab. A buttonhole. L19.

Scaffold-pole. 'The fried potato chip sold with fried fish' (Ware). L19.

Scaly fish. A rough but honest sailor, a Jack Tar. L18–19.

Scamander. Wander round aimlessly. M19.

Scammered. Heavily inebriated. M19.

Scandal-broth. Tea. L18–19.

Scapathy. 'That feeling of depression which, after a while, comes to affect many of the servicemen stationed in the Orkneys' (*Forces' Slang*) (wwii). M20.

Scarborough-warning. One given too late to be any use. M16–L19.

Scarlet horse. A hack, or hired (high-red) horse. L18–M19.

Schemestress. A female trickster (US). E20.

Schitt. A schoolboy term for a goal scored in football. M19.

School butter. The custom of administering a beating to anyone entering school without removing their hat. L18–E19.

Scobolotcher. A student with his hands in his pockets. M16–E20.

Scollogue. Behave especially dissolutely. M–L19.

Scorcher. 1. A reckless cyclist. L19–E20. 2. A rotten potato. L19.

Scot. Any short-tempered individual teased for the purposes of providing entertainment to the group. E–M19.

Scotch. Answer Scotch fashion. Respond to a question with one of one's own. M19. *Scotch bait.* 'A halt and a resting on a stick, as practised by pedlars' (Grose). L18–M19. *Scotch chocolate.* Brimstone and milk. L18–M19. *Scotch mist.* 'A sober soaking rain; a Scotch mist will wet an Englishman to the skin' (Grose). M19–20. *Scotch warming pan.* 1. A woman. M17–L19. 2. A fart. E19–E20.

Scotsman's cinema. The neon advertising displays of Piccadilly Circus. M20.

Scouse. Unpleasantly thin, tasteless stew. E19–E20.

Scrape. Scrape the kettle. Go to confession. L19. *Scrape the pavement.* Shave (US). E20.

Scratch-platter. 'Bread sopped in the oil and vinegar in which cucumbers have been sliced' (Grose). L18–M19.

Screeve. A chalk drawing by a pavement artist. M19.

Screw. Use a skeleton key to obtain access to a building for nefarious purposes. 19.

Scroby, get. Be flogged in front of the magistrates. M19.

Scrongo. A motor car (US). E20.

Scroof. 'A sponge: one who endeavours to live at other people's expense, so that he can save his own pockets' (Egan). M19–E20.

Scroogy. Weird, revolting (US). E20.

Scrousher. A broken-down old gold-prospector (AUS, NZ). M–L19.

Scrubber. 1. A student loner. M–L19. 2. A bullock that has run wild (AUS). M19–M20.

Scud. A very nippy schoolboy. M19. *Scud track.* The dance floor (US). E20.

Scuffle-hunter. A dockyard thief. L18–19.

Scufter. A northern policeman. M–L19.

Scug. 'An untidy or ill-mannered or morally undeveloped boy: a shirker at games' (Partridge). 19–E20.

Scuttle-mouth. A small oyster with a large shell. M19.

Sea. Sea-lawyer. A shark. 19. *Sea-pork.* The meat from a tender young whale. L19–20.

Sebastianist. An incorrigible optimist. L19–E20.

Sedgley curse, i.e. 'may the devil ride through him, booted and spurred, with a scythe on his back'. E17–M19.

See one's grandmother. Have a disturbing nightmare. M19–E20.

Sensation. 1. Half a glass of sherry (AUS). M–L19. 2. A quarter-pint of gin. M–L19.

Sepia sin-spot. A low dive in Harlem. E20.

Sex-appeal bombing. 'The bombing of museums, schools, hospitals – indeed, of civilians in general' (*Forces' Slang*) (WWII). M20.

Shabbaroon. A ragamuffin. L17–19.

Shackles. Soup, or any other food liable to unsettle the bowels (US). E20.

Shack-per-swaw. Every man for himself. M19.

Shag. 1. Chase wrongdoers in order to arrest them (US). E20. 2. Saunter nonchalantly (US). M20.

Shagroon. A retired whaler who settles down with a Maori wife; an interloper from Australia (NZ). M19.

Shakespeare-navels. A 'long-pointed, turned-down collar' (Ware). M–L19.

Shallow. Insufficiently dressed for the weather (usually for the purposes of arousing sympathy). M19.

Sham. An American policeman. E–M20.

Shandygaff. An unsatisfactory compromise. L19–M20.

Shanks's naggy. The Scots precursor to Shanks's pony. M18–19.

She. Queen Victoria (in homage to Rider Haggard). L19.

Shed a tear for Nelson. Urinate. M19.

Sheep. Keep sheep by moonlight. Be hanged in chains. L18–M19. *Sheep-biter.* A butcher. L17–E18. *Sheep-skin fiddler.* A drummer. E–M19.

Shepherd. Place under police surveillance. M–L19.

Shepherd's friend. A dingo (AUS). L19–20.

Sherry. Run off. L18–M19.

Shevvle. A 'genteel designation' for cat food (from the French for 'horse'). M–L19.

Shickster or *Shakester.* A lady. M–L19.

Shifting ballast. Derogatory expression used by sailors for passengers, soldiers or other landsmen on board their ship. L18–M19.

Shilling emetic. 'A pleasure boat at a seaside resort' (Bowen). L19–M20.

Shiny Bob. An Australian with a very high opinion of himself. E–M20.

Shit. 'Heavy shelling and other enemy activity' (*Forces' Slang*) (wwii). M20. *Shit and derision.* Foul, wet weather, making for unpleasant flying conditions (wwii). M20. *Shit-sack.* 1. One meriting the appellation, i.e. 'a dastardly fellow' (Grose). L18–20. 2. A Nonconformist. L18–M19.

Shivering Jemmy. 'The name given by street-folk to any cadger who exposes himself, half naked, on a cold day, to obtain alms' (Hotten). M–L19.

Shoddy-dropper. A pedlar of cheap cloth; a swindler. M20.

Shoe-maker's pride. Shoes which squeak. M19–20.

Shong. A catapult (AUS, NZ). 20.

Shoot. Shoot a bishop. Have a wet dream. M19–E20. *Shoot one's pasteboard.* Call on an acquaintance and leave a visiting card. M19. *Shoot the cat.* Vomit. L18–20.

Short. Neat gin. M19–20. *Short cock.* Yorkshire cheese. E20. *Short-heeled wench.* 'A girl apt to fall on her back' (Grose). L18–E19.

Shotling. A thin pig, bought for fattening up. L17–E18.

Shoulder feast. A dinner for pall-bearers after a funeral. 19.

Shove. Shove a trunk. Barge into a group or place without invitation; gatecrash. L18–L19. *Shove in the mouth.* A dram. E19. *Shove the tumbler.* Be whipped at the cart's tail. L17–E19. *Shoving the moon.* 'Moving goods by moonlight to prevent their being seized by a landlord' (Egan). E–M19.

Shovel bum. A second-rate tramp (US). E20.

Show one's agility. (Of a woman) reveal substantial amounts of one's person when being helped across a stile. L19–E20.

Shrab. 'A favourite drink with the old sailormen who visited Calcutta, as foul a drink as could be imagined' (Bowen); a sweet, non-alcoholic fruit cordial. L19–20.

Shrimp. A prostitute. M17.

Shtumer. 'A horse against which money may be laid without risk' (Hotten); a safe bet. L19.

Sigster. A catnap. M19.

Silent Percy. A rubber gun (q.v.). E20.

Silver-laced. Crawling with lice. E19–E20.

Simkin. Champagne. M–L19.

Simper like a frumety-kettle. Smile, or look jolly. L17–E19.

Singed cat. An undercover police officer (US). E20.

Single-peeper. A monocular man. L18–M19.

Singleton. A corkscrew that works. L18–E19.

Sir. Sir Sydney. A clasp knife. E–M19. *Sir Timothy.* 'One that treats everybody, and pays the reckonings every where' (B.E.). L17–E19. *Sir Walter Scott.* A mug of beer. M19.

Six. Six-and-eightpence. 1. The fee paid to ensure an executed criminal is buried properly. L17–M18. 2. A solicitor. M18. *Six-pounder.* A maid (from her annual wage). L18–M19.

Sizzard. A heat wave (US). E20.

Skeleton army. Street brawling (after an organisation recruited to oppose the rather too muscular Christianity of the early Salvation Army). L19.

Skiboo. An American gunfighter. E20.

Skippy. A police captain in America. E20.

Skolkuring. 'The illegal trading of army food and material to civilians' (*War Slang*) (WWI). E20.

Skookum. In tip-top condition (US). 19–20.

Skweejee. Force one's way through a crowd (US). E20.

Sky. Sky-blue. 1. Gin. M18–M19. 2. Watered down, or over-enthusiastically skimmed, milk. L18–E20. *Sky-farmers.* 'Cheats who pretend they were farmers in the isle of Skye, or some other remote place, and were ruined by a flood, hurricane, or some such public calamity' (Grose). M18–M19. *Sky-larker.* A burglar who disguises himself as a bricklayer. 18–M19. *Sky-pilot.* A clergyman. L19–20. *Sky the wipe.* A hypodermic syringe (US). M20.

Slag. 1. A timid, put-upon man. L18–E19. 2. One who makes use of the free attractions at a fairground while avoiding all the rides and shows charging admission. L19–E20.

Slang-whanger. A long-winded speaker; a user of slang words and phrases in an inappropriate context. E–M19.

Slap. Slap-bang. A cheap restaurant where one pays up front rather than after one has eaten. L18–M19. *Slap-jacks.* Footwear (US). E20. *Slap man.* A plain-clothes policeman (US). E–M20. *Slap the dog-house.* Play the upright bass *con brio* (US). E20.

Sleek and slum shop. 'A public-house or tavern where single men and their wives resort' (Bee). 19.

Sleep. Sleep with Mrs Green. Sleep in the open air (NZ). E–M20. *Sleepy.* (Of fabric) heavily worn, i.e. missing its nap. L18–E19.

Slice. Sliced squeal. Rashers of bacon (US). E20. *Take a slice.* Have an illicit relationship with a married woman. L18–E19.

Sling. Blow one's nose without the assistance of a handkerchief. M–L19. *Sling a slobber.* Bestow a bit more than a peck on the cheek. M19–E20. *Sling the bat.* Speak the local language when stationed abroad. 19–20. *Sling the smash.* Smuggle tobacco into prison. L19.

Slip-slops. A soft drink. 18.

Slosh the burick. Beat one's wife. M–L19.

Slour. Button up one's coat properly. 19.

Slubber-de-gullion. An individual prone to dribbling, or otherwise unhygienic in appearance. E17–19.

Slug. Sluggers. Sloe gin (WWII). M20. *Slug-nutty.* Punch drunk (US). M20.

Sluicery. A gin shop. 19.

Slum. 1. A room. E–M19. 2. Lies, bullshit. E–M19. 3. The sort of cheap jewellery given as fairground prizes. L19–20. 4. Throat lozenges. E–M20.

Slumgullion. 'Any cheap, nasty, washy beverage' (Hotten), from the term's other meaning: fish offal, or the slimy, bloody, liquid refuse from whale blubber. L19.

Slummock. A messy, undomesticated woman (US). E20.

Slush-bucket. A person with a penchant for greasy fried food. L18–M19.

Sluts'-wool. See *Beggars' velvet.*

Smack. Smack calf's skin. Swear an oath (on the Bible). L18–L19. *Smacking-cove.* A coachman. L17–E19.

Smart money. 'Money allowed to soldiers or sailors for the loss of a limb, or other hurt received in the service' (Grose). L18–E19.

Smash. 1. Mashed turnips. L18–M19. 2. Tobacco. L19.

Smellers. A cat's whiskers. M18–19.

Smelling cheat. A garden, or bunch of flowers. M16–L18.

Smigget. A sailor's more attractive crewmate (WWII). M20.

Smiggins. Unpalatable prison soup. 19.

Smirk. A fastidiously dapper person. L17–E19.

Smish. A shirt. E–M19.

Smite. Borrow money from one's university tutor. L18–M19.

Smithfield bargain. A marriage of convenience (after the London meat market). L18–M19.

Smoocher. An unlicensed gold-digger (AUS). M–L19.

Smother a parrot. Knock back a glass of neat absinthe in one go. L19–E20.

Smouch. Dried ash-leaves used to adulterate tea. L18–M19.

Smug. A blacksmith. E17–E18. *Smug-boat.* An opium-runners' ship. M20. *Smug lay.* 'Persons who pretend to be smugglers of lace and valuable articles; these men borrow money of publicans by depositing these goods in their hands: they shortly afterwards decamp, and the publican discovers too late that he has been duped, and, on opening the pretended treasure, he finds trifling articles of no value' (*Lex.Bal.*). E–M19.

Smuggle. Sharpen a pencil at both ends. L19–20. *Smuggling-ken.* A bawdy house. E18–E19.

Snaffle. 1. 'A highwayman that has got booty' (B.E.). L17–18. 2. Bore people to tears with one's conversation. M19–M20.

Snag-catcher. A dentist. L19–E20.

Snaggling. The art or sport of goose-angling. M–L19.

Snake. Snake-charmers. A dance band (wwii). m20. *Snake-tart.* An eel pie. m19–20. See also *Little snakesman.*

Snarley yow. A surly old sea-dog. l19–20.

Snatch cly. A thief who targets women's pockets. l18–19.

Sneaker. A motor-boat used to smuggle illegal immigrants or other contraband into the USA. e20.

Sneeze. Kidnap (us). e20. *Sneeze-lurker.* 'A thief who throws snuff in a person's face, and then robs him' (Hotten). m19. *Sneezing-coffer.* A snuff box. e–m19.

Snick-fadger. A petty thief. m–l19.

Sniffer. A heroine or cocaine addict (us). e–m20.

Snigglefritz. A juvenile delinquent (us). e20.

Snipe-shooter. An American who picks up dog-ends. l19–20.

Sniptious. Discourteously abrupt (us). e20.

Sniv. Hold your tongue! e–m19.

Snoach. Speak with a gratingly nasal intonation. e19.

Snob. A cobbler. l18–19.

Snoddy. A soldier. l19–e20.

Snollygoster. An unscrupulous American politician. m–l19.

Snops or *Snopsy.* American gin. l19.

Snork. 1. An infant Australian or New Zealnder. m20. 2. An Australian sausage. m20.

Snot. 1. A gentleman. m19. 2. An oyster (us). e20. *Snotty.* A naval midshipman. 'This inelegant sobriquet dates from the time when My Lords of the Admiralty decided that midshipmen should wear three buttons on their sleeves, thus preventing the young gentlemen from using their sleeves instead of hand-kerchiefs' (*Forces' Slang*). m19–m20.

Snudge. 'A thief who hides himself under a bed, in order to rob the house' (Grose). m17–e19.

Snuffy. Inebriated. e–m19.

Snuggle-puppy. An affectionately tactile young woman (us). e20.

Soap-suds. Gin and hot water, perked up with a splash of lemon and sugar. e–m19.

Sock. Schoolboys' delicacies. e–m19.

Sockdolager. An exceptionally heavy blow, or unanswerable argument; anything imposing. L19–M20.

Socket-money. 'Money paid for a treat, by a married man caught in an intrigue' (Grose). M18–M19.

Sofa lizard. An individual who prefers staying in to going out at night; a couch potato (US). E20.

Soft tommy. A sailors' term for bread (as opposed to ship's biscuit). L18–L19.

Soldier. Borrow an animal without its owner noticing (AUS). M19–E20.

Solo player. 'A miserable performer on any instrument, who always plays alone, because no one will stay in the room to hear him' (Grose). L18–M19.

Son of a bitch. 'A moustache and imperial whiskers favoured by cattle-buyers and wool inspectors' (Baker, Aus.). L19.

Soothing syrup. Gin. M19.

Sore leg. A plum pudding (from its alarmingly gangrenous appearance). L19.

Soss-brangle. A woman of insalubrious habits. L17–19.

Sound-tosser. A broadcaster on American radio. E20.

South. South jeopardy. The terrors of insolvency suffered by an Oxford undergraduate. M19. *South sea.* Gin. M18–E19. (Also *South sea mountain, South sea sherry.*)

Spange. Smart, dashing. L19.

Spanish. Spanish athlete. A smooth talker (US). E20. *Spanish faggot.* The sun. L18–M19. *Spanish padlock.* A chastity belt. 16–19. *Spanish plague.* Property development. L17–M18. *Spanish worm.* A nail encountered in a plank which one is sawing through. L18–M19. *The Spanish.* Ready money. L18–E19.

Spank the glaze. Smash a window with one's fist. E19.

Spare wank. 'One with no definite job to do' (*Forces' Slang*) (WWII). M20.

Sparrow. A milkman's special customer. L19–E20. *Sparrow-mouth.* 'One whose mouth cannot be enlarged without removing their ears' (Grose). L17–E20.

Speckled wipe. A coloured handkerchief. L17–L19.

Speedball. A powerful cocktail comprising port wine with a shot of ether floated on top (US). E–M20.

Spell baker. Attempt something tricky. 18–19.

Spencer. An undersized glass of gin. E–M19.

Spider. Claret and lemonade. L19–E20.

Spiflicate or *Smifligate.* 1. Flabbergast. L18–20. 2. Grievously assault or kill. L18–20. 3. Often used as an obscure but disturbing threat to children. L19–20.

Spike. A High Church Anglican clergyman. L19–E20. *Spike bozzle.* Pursue an enemy aircraft (US: WWI). E20.

Spin a cuffer. Recount an implausible story. L19–20.

Spinikin. A workhouse. M19.

Spit amber. 'Expectorate while chewing tobacco' (Ware) (US). M–L19.

Spitchered. Completely broken or destroyed (WWII). M20.

Split. A half-bottle of mineral water. L19. *Split-arsing.* Low-level acrobatics; buzzing the huts near an airfield (WWI). E20. *Split-fig.* A grocer. L17–E19.

Splodger. A country bumpkin. M19.

Spoffskins. An escort-girl willing to pose as her client's wife. L19–E20.

Spoffy. Officious busybodying. M19.

Spoil pudding. A parson with an unfortunate predilection for excessively long sermons on Sunday mornings. L18–M19.

Spoon-holder. A comfortably padded window-seat (US). E20.

Sport. Sport a nescio. Deliberately fail to understand something. E19. *Sport blubber.* 'Said of a large coarse woman, who exposes her bosom' (*Lex.Bal.*). L18–20.

Spout Billy. Earn a meagre living by reciting Shakespeare badly in pubs. 19.

Spuddy. A seller of poor potatoes. M19.

Spunk. 'Rotten touchwood, or a kind of fungus prepared for tinder; figuratively, spirit, courage' (Grose). L18–L19. *Spunk-fencer.* A match-seller. M–L19. *Spunk up.* Be roused to anger or action (US). E20.

Spuzzy. Snug (us). E20.

Squandary. The uncomfortable financial predicament caused by one's over-lavish lifestyle (us). E20.

Square. Square-face. Gin. L19. *Square Jane and no nonsense.* 'A firm-minded girl of conservative instincts' (Baker, Aus.). E–M20. *Square-pusher.* A soldier's girlfriend. E–M20. *Square-toes.* An old man (from their preserving the fashion in their youth for square-toed shoes). L18–M19.

Squash ballad. An ardently patriotic song. L19–E20.

Squatocracy. Office workers (us). E20.

Squeeker. A youthful carrier pigeon (us). E20.

Squiffer. A concertina. L19–E20.

Squinkies. Short films (us). E–M20.

Squirrel. 1. 'A prostitute: because she, like that animal, covers her back with her tail' (*Lex.Bal.*). L18–M19. 2. A psychologist (us). M20. See also *Hunt the squirrel.*

Squish. Marmalade; also preserves more generally. L19–20.

Stale drunk. Hung-over. 19.

Stallion. 'A man kept by an old lady for secret services' (Grose). L17–19.

Stand. Stand Moses. 'A man is said to stand Moses when he has an-other man's bastard child fathered upon him, and he is obliged by the parish to maintain it' (*Lex.Bal.*). L18–E19. *Stand the huff.* To pay the bill in a pub. L18–L19. *Stand the patter.* Be put on trial. E19. *Stand upon one's pantables.* Stand on one's dignity. M16–M18.

Star. Star-gazer. A 'hedge whore'. L18–M19. *Stars and stripes.* Pork and beans (us). L19–20.

Stark naked. Gin. 19. (Also *Staff naked, Strip me naked.*)

Starve the bardies. A Western Australian variation on 'Stone the crows' (*bardies* are wood grubs). M20.

Steam. Steam-engine. A Lancashire potato pie. M19. *Steamer.* Stewed kangaroo with pork (aus). L19–20.

Stellenbosched. Be relieved of one's duties and posted back home (wwi). E20.

Stenogunist. A mobster with a machine gun (us). E–M20.

Stepfatherland. One's adopted country (us). E20.

Stereo. Very old news. L19.

Sterling. A British-born emigrant to Australia. 19.

Stewed Quaker. An American cold remedy: burnt rum with a knob of butter dissolved in it. L18–E19.

Stibber-gibber. An individual with a very relaxed attitude to the truth. M16.

Stick-flams. A pair of gloves. L17–19.

Stiff. Stiff-fencer. A writing-paper hawker. M19. *Stiffy.* An American beggar who attempts to arouse sympathy by pretending to be paralysed. E20.

Stifle the squeaker. Dispose of an illegitimate child. L17–E20.

Stinkious. Gin. 18.

Stodge. Stuff oneself with food to the point of exhaustion. M–L19.

Stonkered. In a sticky situation or predicament (NZ: WWI, WWII). E–M20.

Stop thief. A piece of pilfered meat. M19.

Straddle. Decide who pays a bill by cutting cards, etc. 18.

Straight-drinking. The consumption of alcohol while standing at the bar. M19–E20. *Straight-hair.* 1. Western Australian term for a convict. M19. 2. A Western Australian. L19.

Strain one's taters. Urinate. L19.

Stretching bee. A hanging. E19–E20.

Strike-fire. Gin. E–M18.

Strill polone. A female pianist. L19–20.

Stringy-bark. An ingenious blend of fuel-oil and turpentine sold as 'whisky' (AUS). L19–E20.

Strong and thin. Gin (us). E–M20. (Also *Thick and thin.*)

Struggle-buggy. An American student's motor car. M20.

Strum. 1. Have vigorous sex with a woman. L18–19. 2. Play the harpsichord badly. L18–E19.

Stugging. The unsettling motion of a ship that has run aground. L19–20.

Stumble at the truckle bed. Absent-mindedly find oneself in the maid's bed instead of one's wife's. M17–M18.

Sublime rascal. A lawyer. 19.

Suck. Suck-casa. A public house. M19–20. *Suck one's face.* Drink. L17–M18. *Suck the monkey.* 1. Illicitly drink from a sealed cask using a straw. L18. 2. Drink rum out of a coconut. E–M19. See also *Anti-guggler. Suck the mop.* Be the victim of nursing (q.v.). L19. *Sucker.* An immature whale. E19. *Sucky.* Maudlin drunk. L17–19.

Suffolk bang. A notoriously hard cheese, but economical. 19.

Sugar. Give the appearance of rowing harder than one actually is. L19. *Sugar-baby.* A child who hates being made to play in the garden or go for a walk when it's raining. L19–20. *Sugar-stick.* The male member. L18–20.

Suicide. 'Four horses driven in a line' (Hotten). M–L19. *Suicide blonde.* An amateurishly dyed blonde (US). E20.

Sunday. Sunday dog. A work-shy sheep- or cattle-dog (NZ). L19–20. *Sunday man.* 'One who goes abroad on that day only, for fear of arrests' (Grose). L18–M19.

Superstitious-pie. A Puritan's mince-pie. L17–M18.

Surf. A 'resting' actor; one 'who frequently pursues another calling' (Hotten). M–L19. *Surf-hurdling.* 'The practice of landing goods from ship to shore in an open boat on an exposed coast-line' (Baker NZ). M20.

Swack-up. A falsehood. M19–20.

Swak. Censor servicemen's mail (WWII). M20.

Swallow the dick. Attempt to impress by using long words when one does not know their meaning. M–L19. See *Dick.*

Swamp. Swamp gaboon. The fantastical beast believed responsible for the tracks left by snowshoes (US). E20. *Swamp seed.* Rice (US). E20.

Swatfest. Golf played by women; a not very good game of golf (US). E20.

Sweet. Sweet-heart. A pet rabbit (from its calculating furry cuteness). M19. *Sweet waters.* 'Illicit spirit made from the residue of the cider press. Fearfulest drink in the world' (Ware). M19–E20.

Swell. Take a bath. M19.

Swimmer. Sentence a criminal to a stint in the navy instead of a term in prison. M19.

Swindle. A lottery. M–L19.

Swing it across the desert. Obtain admission to hospital under false pretences while serving in the Middle East (WWI). E20.

Swot. A mathematician. M–L19.

Sydney duck. A disreputable Australian participant in the California Gold Rush of 1849 (US, AUS). M–L19.

System d. Take an unorthodoxly direct approach to resolving an apparently intractable problem. E–M20.

Table-end man. 'A husband whose desires are so urgent that he cannot wait to go upstairs' (Partridge). L19–20.

Tack wallah. A military teetotaller. L19–E20.

Tail-pulling. Vanity publishing. L19–E20.

Talk. Talk packthread. Lard one's conversation with double entendres. L18–E19. *Talk turpentine.* Discuss art with at least the pretence of knowledgeability. L19. *Talk wet.* 'Talk that comes out of the mouth accompanied by beer or saliva' (Soldierman), i.e. not worth listening to. E–M20.

Tall 'un. A pint of coffee. L19–20.

Tally. Tally-ho. The situation of a kept or cohabiting woman. L19–E20. *Tally-man.* A hirer of clothes to prostitutes. L18–E19.

Tamarboo. A cab-driver. M19.

Tangerine. A person imprisoned for debt. L18–E19.

Tannhäuser. The penis (after the opera's enlargement in 1861). M–L19.

Tantivy-boy. A staunch Tory or High Churchman. L17–M18.

Tap-lash. Glutinously substandard beer. E17–E19.

Tarry rope. An Australian woman who spends time down at the docks doing favours for sailors. M20.

Tatter a kip. Trash a brothel by way of a jape. M18–M19.

Tea. Tea-bottle. An old maid. L19–E20. *Tea-kettle coachman.* A male servant in a small, middle-class establishment, expected to look after the garden, the coach, and a variety of other general tasks. M–L19. *Tea-pot soak.* A collector of other people's tea-pots. M–L19. *Tea-spoon.* £5,000. M19. *Tea-voider.* A chamber pot. L18–L19.

Teddy bear. A particularly woolly fur coat (WWI). E20.

Tee-whop. Make one's girlfriend laugh out loud. E19.

Telescope. Shut someone up (AUS). L19–E20.

Tender parnel. A sensitive plant, a wimp. L17–E19.

Ten in the hundred. A usurer (more than five per cent interest being usurious). L16–L18.

Terp. Dance (after the Muse, Terpsichore) (US). E20.

Terra firma. An estate in the country. L17–E19.

Thatch-gallows. A rogue, villain or other undesirable. L18–M19.

Thimble-crib. A watchmaker's shop. E–M19.

Thingstable. A constable. 'A ludicrous affectation of delicacy in avoiding the pronunciation of the first syllable in the title of that officer, which in sound has some similarity to an indecent monosyllable' (Grose). L18–E19.

Thorough cough. 'Coughing and breaking wind backwards at the same time' (Grose). L17–E19.

Thousand-mile shirt. A luridly coloured shirt (i.e. so bright it is visible at a great distance); or a dark, hard-wearing one which doesn't show the dirt (US). E20.

Three. Three-figure man. A criminal with a £100 reward on his head. M19–E20. *Three-penny upright.* A 'retailer of love' who dispenses economical knee-tremblers. L18–19. *365.* Bacon and eggs for breakfast (every day). L19–E20.

Throw an ing-bing. Go insane (US). E20.

Thumb-buster. An old-fashioned revolver (US). E20.

Thunder. Clap of thunder. A glass of gin. E–M19. *Thunder and lightning.* 1. Gin and bitters. 19–20. 2. A treacle and clotted-cream sandwich. L19. See also *Blood and thunder*; *Duck in a thunderstorm, like a.*

101

Thunkard. An individual whose mental exertions have reduced him to a stupor (US). E20.

Tickle. Tickle one's toby. Thrash someone's buttocks. L17–M19. *Tickle-pitcher.* A drinking companion, or 'toss-pot'. L17–E19. *Tickler's.* An improvised hand-grenade, made out of a (Tickler's) jam tin (WWI). E20.

Tiddle a girl. Seduce a woman very gently. M19–E20.

Tiddly. Tiddly-suit. A sailor's best uniform. E–M20. *Tiddly-wink.* 1. Any unlicensed establishment: a brothel, pawnbroker, pub, etc. M19. 2. Squander one's money (AUS). L19.

Tiffing. 'Eating or drinking out of meal times' (Grose). L18–E19.

Tiger. Streaky bacon. L19–E20. *Tiger's milk.* Gin. M–L19.

Tiggy. A detective. L19–E20.

Tiled. Comfortably snug (i.e. with a weather-proof roof over one's head). E–M19.

Tilladumite. A hand-loom weaver. M19.

Tillicum. A friend, acquaintance or relative (US). E20.

Timber-toe. 1. A man with a wooden leg. L18–E20. 2. A clog-wearer. L19–E20.

Timmynoggy. Any labour-saving device onboard ship. M–L19.

Tin. Tin-arsed. Fantastically lucky (AUS: WWI). E20. *Tin lizzie.* A Ford automobile (WWI). E20. *Tin pants.* Heavy-duty waterproof trousers favoured by lumberjacks (US). E20. *Tin shin off.* Abscond with the money from a robbery or fraud (US). L19.

Tinny-hunters. 'Persons whose practice it is to attend fires, for the purpose of plundering the unfortunate sufferers, under the pretence of assisting them to remove their property' (Egan). L18–E19.

Tip. Tip the auctioneer. Deliver a knock-down punch. M18–E20. *Tip the lion.* Squash someone's nose and either poke him in the eyes or pull his lips apart with one's fingers. E18–M19. *Tip the traveller.* Tell fantastical tales. M18–M19. *Tip the velvet.* 1. French kiss someone. L17–L19. 2. Tell a person off. E–M19.

Tisket. A bastard (WWII). M20.

Tit. A student at Durham university. L19–20.

Titotular bosh. Complete and utter nonsense. L19.

Titter. A flighty young woman. E19–E20.

Tittery. Gin. E–M18.

Toad. Sit like a toad upon a chopping block. Ride a horse inelegantly. L18–E19. *Toad-eater.* 'A poor female relation, an humble companion, or reduced gentlewoman in a great family, the standing butt, on which all kinds of practical jokes are played off, and all ill humours vented' (Grose). L18–E19. *Toad-skins.* Banknotes (US, AUS). E20.

Toast. The devil. L17–L19.

Tober omee. A toll-collector or roadside pub landlord. L19.

Toff. Toffer. A classy call-girl, one who 'does' toffs. M19–E20. *Toff-shoving.* The sport of 'pushing about well-dressed men in a crowd' (Ware). L19.

Togie. A short length of rope employed for chastising young sailors. L19–E20.

Toko for yam. A fair exchange. L19.

Tom. 'A masculine woman of the town. In higher ranks one who does not care for the society of others than those of her own sex' (Ware). M19–E20. *Tom-and-Jerry.* Behave riotously. E–M19. *Tomfoolery.* 'Trashy, mild, and innocuous literature' (Hotten). M19. *Tommy.* Work for payment in kind. M19. *Tommy Dodd.* A revolver (US). E–M20. *Tom the tanks.* Tour the small towns of America with a production of *Uncle Tom's Cabin.* L19–E20.

Tombstone. A pawn ticket. M19.

Tonguer. An early white inhabitant of New Zealand given to dismembering whales in order to earn a living. 19.

Ton of law. A very large policeman (US). E20.

Tool. 'A very little boy employed by burglars to enter at small apertures, and open doors for the larger thieves outside' (Hotten). M19–E20.

Tooth-music. Mastication. L18–E19.

Toot one's own bazoo. Talk oneself up, blow one's own trumpet (US). E20.

Too utterly too-too. Very much. L19.

Top ballocks. A woman's breasts. L19–20.

Topper-hunter. An individual who smokes or sells dog-ends. M19–E20.

Torso-tosser. An American theatrical dancer. E20.

Tory democracy. 'Impossibility' (Ware). L19.

Tosh. A waterproof coat, a mac. E20. *Tosher.* A man who steals the copper sheathing off ships' bottoms in the Thames. M19.

Tosser. A baseball player (US). E20.

Tot. Tot-picker. A rag and bone man. M–L19. *Tot-sack.* The bag in which a soldier keeps his rations (WWI). E20.

Totty. Totty-headed. Hare-brained. L18–E19. *Totty one-lung.* 'An asthmatic, or consumptive young person who … thinks herself somebody' (Ware). L19.

Tower-Hill-play. 'A slap on the face, and a kick on the breech' (B.E.). L17–18.

Town. Town bull. A sexually promiscuous man, 'one that rides all the women he meets' (B.E.). L17–19. *Town clown.* A village policeman (US). M20.

Towzery-gang. 'Swindlers who hire sale-rooms, usually in the suburbs, for mock auction sales of cheap and worthless goods, and who advertise their ventures as "Alarming Sacrifices", "Important Sales of Bankrupts' Stock", etc.' (Hotten). M–L19.

Tradesman. A thief. 19.

Translate. Translate the truth. Attempt to put a positive spin on something; lie evasively. L19. *Translator.* A seller of refurbished second-hand footwear. L17–M19.

Travelling circus. A WWI mobile machine-gun unit; also an inspection at the front by top brass. Both loathed by soldiers for the disruption they create. E20.

Trench. US soldiers' slang of WWI, much of it derived from bad puns and corrupted French (hence the name). E20.

Triangles. Delirium tremens, 'during a fit of which everything appears out of the square' (Hotten). M19

Trigrymate. A good-for-nothing female companion. L17–19.

Trig the jigger. Enter a temporarily unoccupied house and steal its contents and fittings. E19.

Trilby. A foot, especially if a woman's and alluring. L19–E20.

Trinity kiss. Kisses given by young children to their parents when sent off to bed. L19.

Tripes and trullibubs. A cheerily derogatory term for a fat man, or porker. L18–L19.

Trojan. A professional gambler. E–M19.

Trolly. Trolly-lolly. Unfashionable cheap lace. L17–E19. *Trolly-wags.* Trousers. L19.

Trotter-boxes. Footwear. 19.

Trouser. A jack of all trades. L19.

Trundlers. Peas. M17–M19.

Trunkmaker-like. Producing more noise than work. L18–M19.

Trusty trout. A true friend. M17–M19.

Tube train. A large shell rumbling safely overhead (WWI). E20.

Tubs. Sufferers from tuberculosis (US). E20.

Tum-tum. A dog-cart. M–L19.

Tune the old cow died of. A ghastly noise; a horribly played, or just plain bad, piece of music. M19.

Tunnel-grunters. Potatoes. L19–E20.

Tupper. 'A commonplace honest bore' (Ware). M–L19.

Turk. An Irishman (US). M19–E20. *Turkish shore.* The benighted region south of the river in London. L17–E19.

Turn. Turn stag. Inform on one's confederates, grass up one's mates. L18–M19. *Turn-up.* A brawl, or informal boxing match. E19.

Turnip-pated. Blond, or white-haired. L17–19.

Turnpike-man. 'A parson, because the clergy collect their tolls at our entrance into and exit from the world' (Grose). L18–M19.

Turtle frolic. A feast of turtle. L18.

Twack. Browse without buying anything from a shop in Newfoundland. 19–E20.

Twang. 1. 'Engage in spontaneous sexual intercourse' (Green). 17–18. 2. Opium (AUS). L19–M20.

Twankey. Gin. L19–E20.

Tweaguey. In a tizz. L18–E19.

Tweak. Hit someone (or -thing) with a catapult. L19.

Twiddle. Twiddle-diddles. Testicles. L18–E19. *Twiddle-poop.* An effeminate man. L18–M19.

Twillip. A stupid or unpleasant acquaintance; an annoying jerk (WWII). M20.

Twist. 1. An appetising confection of tea and coffee. L17–E18. 2. A mellow blend of brandy and gin. M19.

Twitzy pretzel. Someone peculiar (US). E20.

Twixter. 'A lady-like young man, or a man-like young woman' (Partridge). L19–E20.

Two. Two-acre back. A substantial woman bedizened with too much heavy jewellery. L19–E20. *Two-eyed steak.* A kipper. L19–M20. *Two-to-one shop.* A pawnbroker's. L18–M19. *Two whoops and a holler.* Near by (US). E20.

Tyburn. Tyburn blossom. 'A young thief or pickpocket, who in time will ripen into fruit borne upon the deadly never-green' (*Lex.Bal.*). L18–M19. *Tyburn top.* 'A wig with the foretop combed over the eyes in a knowing style' (*Lex.Bal.*). L18–E19. *Wear Tyburn tiffany.* Be hanged. E17–18.

Typerighter. An American proofreader. E20.

Typewriter. A machine gun. E–M 20.

Tzing-tzing. Absolutely the bee's knees. L19.

Ullage. Wine left in the bottom of glasses at a party, secretly drunk by the waiters. L19.

Umpty poo. A smidgeon more (cf. *un petit peu*) (WWI). E20.

Unbetty. Unlock. E–M19.

Uncertainty. A baby girl. L19.

Uncle, go to visit one's. Abandon one's wife soon after marriage. L18–19.

Under-dubber. A prison warder, or gaoler. 19.

Undigested Ananias. A shockingly unrepentant liar. L19–E20.

Universal staircase. A prison treadmill. M19–E20.

Un-palled. 'One whose companions have all been either hanged or transported' (Egan). 19.

Unsweetened. Gin. M–L19.

Upright. Beer enriched with gin. L18–19. *Upright man.* The head of a criminal gang. M16–E19. *Upright sneak.* 'One who steals pewter pots from the alehouse boys employed to collect them' (*Lex.Bal.*). L18–E20. See also *Three-penny upright.*

Urinal of the planets. Ireland, 'because of its frequent and great rains, as Heidelberg and Cologne in Germany have the same name upon the same account' (B.E.). L17–M19.

Vamper. A member of a gang of thieves, one of whom picks fights with conspicuously well-to-do pub-goers while the other steals their valuables in the confusion. M19.

Vampire. An insufferably boring person (because they drain one of the will to live). M19.

Vamps. Re-footed socks. E–M19.

Varm. 'The exasperating quintessence of the female sex' (Weseen) (US). E20.

Varmint-man. A professional essay-writer for lazy students. M–L19.

VC mixture. Rum (WWI). E20.

Vegetable breakfast. A hanging. L19.

Velveteens. A gamekeeper. M–L19.

Vera Lynn. Gin. M20.

Vespasian. A public convenience. L19–E20.

Vestal. 'An incontinent woman' (Bee); a right slapper. E19.

Vice Admiral of the Narrow Seas. 'A drunken man that pisses under the table into his companions' shoes' (*Lex. Bal.*). 17–E19. See *Admiral of the Narrow Seas.*

Vincent. The victim of crooked gamblers. L16–18.

Virgins' bus. The last bus west from Piccadilly Circus. M–L19.

Voluntary knee-drill. Ecstatic adoration. L19.

Wabbler. 1. A boiled leg of mutton (from the noise it makes in the pot). E–M19. 2. A pedestrian. M19–E20.

Waddle out of the Alley. Said of a stockbroker unable or unwilling to pay his creditors. M18–L19.

Waddy. 1. A walking stick (AUS). l19–20. 2. A capable cowboy or seasonal hired hand; among thieves, an all-round good egg (US). E20.

Wad-scoffer. A military teetotaller (WWI). E20.

Wagga blanket. A tramp's bedclothes (AUS). L19–20.

Walking distiller. 'One who carries the keg', i.e. an irritable individual whose nose is easily put out of joint. 19.

Wall. Wall-chalker. One who daubs graffiti or scrawls advertising slogans on to street walls. E19. *Wall-flower.* An item of second-hand clothing sold on the street. E–M19.

Wallaby-track, on the. Take to the road in Australia in search of employment. M19–20.

Walloper. A dancer. M–L19.

Wally. 1. A pickled cucumber. L19–20. 2. A gambler from small-town America. E20.

Wallyford. A three-and-a-half-mile run on a wet school day. L19–M20.

Wampas winner. A child filmstar (US). E20.

Wanky. Fake, defective, i.e. just plain wrong. E20.

Wap. 'A species of slap, resounding, as if imparted by a wet dishclout' (Bee). E–M19.

Wapper-eyed. Blind drunk. E19.

War baby. A surprisingly young-looking soldier (WW1). E20.

Wasp. A prostitute with a venereal infection (who therefore has a 'sting in her tail'). L18–M19.

Water. Water-bewitched. 'Tea fit only for husbands to sip' (Bee). L17–E19. *Water of life.* Gin. M19. *Water the dragon.* Urinate. M19.

Watermeloncholy. The craving for watermelons (US). E20.

Wattles. Ears. L18–M19.

Waxy-homey. An unconvincing actor who blacks up with burnt cork. L19.

Wear. Wear one's sitting breeches. Out-stay one's welcome at a party. E19–E20. *Wear the willow.* Be dumped by a lover or mistress. L16–E19.

Weary Willie. An artillery shell appearing to move very slowly because high overhead (WW1). E20.

Weaving. 'A notorious card-sharping trick, done by keeping certain cards on the knee, or between the knee and the underside of the table, and using them when required by changing them for the cards held in the hand' (Hotten). 19.

Wedding. The process of emptying a privy. L18–E19.

Weed. Steal a small amount from a large quantity (e.g. from a warehouse or out of a shop till), either out of fear or to maximise the potential takings over time. E19.

Weejee. 1. A chimney-pot. M–L19. 2. A brilliant idea or invention. M–L19.

Welsh. Welsh comb. A hand. L18–M19. *Welsh ejectment.* The eviction of a tenant by removing his roof – apparently a common practice in Wales. E–M19. *Welsh rabbit.* Cheese on toast. 'The Welsh are said to be so remarkably fond of cheese, that in cases of difficulty their midwives apply a piece of toasted cheese to the *janua vitae* to attract and entice the young Taffy, who on smelling it makes most vigorous efforts to come forth' (Grose). E18–20.

Westminster wedding. 'A whore and a rogue married together' (B.E.). L17–E19.

Wet. Wet arse and no fish. An unsuccessful errand or unavailing search. L19–E20. *Wet dream.* A dull, dozy school-fellow. L19–20. *Wet soul.* One who journeys through life in a state of near-constant mild inebriation. E–M19. *Wet-thee-through.* Gin. M19.

Whale. A sardine. L19.

Whapper. An unusually large person of either sex. L18–19.

Wheelbarrow. An Australian conscripted into the armed forces (because he has to be pushed) (AUS: WWII). M20.

Whiffle. Whiffle-poof. A complete and utter good-for-nothing (US). E20. *Whiffles.* 'A relaxation of the scrotum' (Grose). L18–M19.

Whig. A spineless, vacillating individual. M19.

Whindle. Feigned crying, crocodile tears. L17–E18.

Whip. Whip-jack. A beggar who impersonates a shipwrecked sailor to arouse pity. M16–L19. *Whipshire.* Yorkshire. L17–18. *Whip-the-cat.* A tailor, carpenter, etc., who makes home visits in order to carry out commissions. E–M19.

Whirlygigs. Testicles. L17–E19.

Whisker. A stupendous untruth. M17–20. *Whisker-splitter.* 'A man of intrigue' (*Lex.Bal.*). L18–M19.

Whisky-stall. An end-of-row seat at the theatre, giving one an advantage in the race to the bar at the interval. L19–E20.

Whistler. Obscure (of doctrines, arguments, conversation, etc.; from the artist's characteristically veiled style). L19.

Whistling-shop. An unlicensed drinking den. E–M19.

White. Arrested by the white sergeant. Dragged out of a public house by one's wife. L18–L19. *Be white-horsed in.* Be appointed to a position through influence rather than on merit. L19. *White-bait.* Silver. E19. *White eye.* 'A very strong and deleterious kind of whisky, so called because its potency is believed to turn the eyes round in the sockets, leaving the whites only visible'

(Hotten). M19. *White face*. Australian gin. E–M19. *White lady*. A heady tipple of methylated spirits and ammonia (AUS). M20. *White line*. Raw alcohol (US). E20. *White tape*. Gin. E18–E19. (Also *White lace*, *White port*, *White ribbon*, *White satin*, *White wine*, *White wool*. L18–E20.)

Whitechapel. When the outcome of a wager is decided on the best of three attempts. M19.

Whittle-whanging. Bickering amongst cowboys (US). E20.

Whockerjawed. Squint (US). E20.

Whoopee. *Whoopee-mama*. 'A flighty young woman … pursuing a lifestyle as far as possible removed from that desired by her parents' (Green). L19–M20. *Whoopee-water*. Potent alcoholic drink (US). E20.

Whooper-dooper. 1. A riotous celebration (US). E–M20. 2. A kitchen hand (US). E–M20.

Whoop up. Tune one's musical instrument before playing (US). L19.

Whopcacker. An expression denoting supreme excellence or superlative qualities (AUS, NZ). E–M20.

Whore-monger. 'A man that keeps more than one mistress' (*Lex.Bal.*). 17–19.

Whow ball. A milkmaid. L17–E19.

Whuff. Bellow like a rhinoceros. L19.

Whyms. Members of the YMCA. L19–E20.

Wibble. Inferior liquor, or any weak drink, e.g. gin. L18–L19.

Wido. A Glaswegian hooligan. L19–20.

Widow. *Grass widow*. An abandoned mistress. 16–E19. *Widow bewitched*. A woman whose husband has vanished and is believed dead, but for which there is no concrete evidence. L18–E19.

Wife. A leg shackle. E–M19. *Wife in water colours*. A mistress ('water colours being, like their engagements, easily effaced or dissolved'). L18–M19.

Wiffle-woffles. A state of pronounced melancholy. E–M19.

Wig. 'Post a scout on the route of … a pigeon race with a hen pigeon, to attract the opponent's bird and retard his progress' (Partridge). M–L19.

Wiganowns. The wearer of a conspicuously large wig. L18–E19.

Wild-cat's ankle. A term of strong approval amongst lumberjacks (US). E20.

Willing tit. A happy little horse. L17–E19.

Willy. Willy boy. 'A dandified young man' (US). E20. *Willy-willy.* A whirlwind (AUS). L19–20.

Wind. 1. Gin. M18. 2. A man transported for life. E19. *Wind-jammer.* 1. An unpopular army officer; one liable to reject his soldiers' requests for leave (WWI). E20. 2. A teller of far-fetched stories (US). E20.

Wing-ding. A feigned fit (US). M20.

Winkle-pin. A jocular term for a bayonet (WWI). E20.

Wino. An itinerant grape-picker or vineyard-worker (US). E20.

Winter's day, like a. 'Short and nasty' (Egan). L18–M19.

Wistycastor. A winding blow delivered by a proficient pugilist. E–M19.

Witch-cove. A wizard. 18–19.

Wiwi or *Wee-wee.* A Frenchman. M18–E20.

Wobble-shop. An unlicensed establishment selling alcohol. M19.

Woffle. Eat, or drink. E–M19.

Wolly. An olive. L19–E20.

Womble. 1. An uneasy roiling in the stomach; nausea. L17–18. 2. Walk with a rolling gait. M19.

Womblety-cropped. The unsettled sensation in one's stomach that accompanies a bad hangover. L17–E19.

Wonk. An incompetent or untrained sailor. L19–20.

Woobles. Stupidity (US). E20.

Wood. Wood butcher. An incompetent carpenter. L19–E20. *Wood pussy.* A polecat (US). E20.

Woodcock. 'A tailor with a long bill' (Grose). L18–E19.

Woofits. A nerve-jangling hangover (US). E20.

Wool. Wool-bird. A sheep. L18–M19. *Wool-hole.* A workhouse. M19–E20. *Woolly.* Exasperated or irritated. M19.

Woop. Woop-knacker. A hard man (NZ). E–M20. *Woop-woop.* The remote rural areas of Australia; the outback. E20.

Wop. Any foreigner, excluding British, French or Germans (US). L19–E20.

Wopple-jaw. A large, jutting chin (US). E20.

Wop-wop. An itinerant sheep-station hand (AUS). E20.

Word. Word-grubber. An individual who lards his conversation with difficult words – an incorrigible sesquipedalianist. L18–M19. *Word of mouth, drink by.* Drink from the bottle rather than out of a glass. L18–M19.

Work. Work-bench. A bedstead. E–M19. *Work for the dead horse,* i.e. for wages that have already been paid. 17–E20. *Work the pea.* (Of bar staff) rob the landlord by pocketing small sums of money from the till. M19. *Work under the arm-pits.* Indulge in minor thievery for which the punishment is transportation (rather than hanging). 19.

Worm. A policeman. M19. *On the worm.* Involved in the silk-stealing business (US). E20.

Worrocks. Watch out! (US) M–L19.

Wouf-hong. An unidentified implement employed for the chastisement of radio hams (US). E20.

Wowser. 'A bald-headed, bad-breathed, bible-banging bummer, who ought to be banged with a bowser' (AUS, NZ). L19–20.

Wrinkler. An inveterate liar. E19.

Wrist-watch. Posh; affectedly smart; effeminate. E20.

Wusser. A canal boat. L19.

Wuzzer. Anything or anyone hopelessly old-fashioned (US). E20.

X. A lavatory (US). E20. *Take X.* Employ an arm-lock to subdue someone resisting arrest. M19.

Xaroshie. A soldiers' expression of satisfaction, frequently mispronounced (WWI). E20.

X-chasers. 'Mathematically minded naval officers' (*Forces' Slang*) (WWII). M20.

X division. Law-breakers and other low-lives; the criminal classes. L19.

X-legged. Knock-kneed. M–L19.

X-ray. A $10,000 note (US). E20.

XYZ. A fop (because, when pronounced in a suitably supercilious and drawling manner, it sounds vaguely like 'exquisite'). E19.

Yaffle. Eat. L18–E19.

Yah-for-yes-folk. Germans or Dutchmen. L19–20.

Yank. (Of British women) pick up American servicemen (WWII). M20. *Yankee.* A cheat or swindler (US). M19–E20. *Yankee paradise.* Paris. M–L19.

Yarmouth. Completely mad (WWII). M20.

Yawptologist. A cheerleader (US). E20.

Yegg. An itinerant thief who targets small-town banks and railroad depots (after the first safe-cracker to employ nitro-glycerine) (US). L19–E20. *Yegg job.* An incompetently handled robbery, or viciously violent act. E20.

Yellow peril. A cheap cigarette (WWI). E20.

YMCA. Priggish (US). L19–E20.

York. Stare aggressively at someone. E–M19.

Yorkshire. Cheat or deceive someone. L19. *Yorkshire reckoning.* A bill settled by everyone paying a share. M19.

Youbetcherland. The backwoods and rural hinterland of the United States of America (US). E20.

Yowler. A turbot. L19–E20.

Yoxter. A transported convict who unlawfully returns to Britain before the end of his sentence. M–L19.

Yuk. A prison pal or cell-mate (US). E20.

Zad. A deformed person or thing. E18–M19.

Zagger. An inexpensive wristwatch (US). E20.

Zdrást! A common greeting between soldiers, from the Russian salutation, *Zdrástvitye,* 'Be healthy' (WWI). E20.

Zedland. 'Great part of the west country, where the letter Z is substituted for S; as zee for see, zun for sun, etc., etc. This prevails through the counties of Devonshire, Dorsetshire, and Somersetshire' (*Lex.Bal.*). L18–19.

Zeppelins in a cloud. Sausage and mash (WWI). E20.

Ziff. 1. An immature thief. M19. 2. An Australian's beard. E20.

Zings. Delirium tremens (US). E20.

Zits. An American false-beard wearer. E20.

Znees or *Znuz.* Frozen. L18–M19. *Zneesy weather.* Frosty. M18–M19.

Zook. 1. An item of confectionery. L19–20. 2. An old, worn-out prostitute (US). E–M20.

Zooner. An aggressive hustler (US). E20.

Zopissa. 'Tar or pitch scraped off old ship, once regarded as a sovereign cure for ulcers' (Bowen). L19.

Zowie. So on and so forth; etcetera, etcetera; blah, blah, blah, blah, blah (US). E20.

Zucke. A decayed tree stump. L18–E19.